BOX LACROSSE
The Fastest Game on Two Feet

THE AUTHOR

Jim Hinkson is outstandingly qualified to write the first full text on box lacrosse. He has played on several championship teams, among them the Oshawa Green Gaels of junior lacrosse fame, the Brooklin Redmen and Windsor Warlocks, senior teams, and the Detroit Olympics and Peterborough Lakers in the professional ranks. An enthusiastic student of the game, he has a unique insight into its mechanics and fundamentals and a particular interest in the theory of team play.

Hinkson currently teaches physical education in an Ontario high school. He has coached lacrosse at both junior and senior levels, and he continues to be active as a player.

BOX LACROSSE

The Fastest Game on Two Feet

Jim Hinkson

Introduction by Jim Bishop

CHILTON BOOK COMPANY
Radnor, Pennsylvania

First American Edition   1975
Copyright © 1974 by James D. Hinkson
First Edition   *All Rights Reserved*

Published in Radnor, Pa., by Chilton Book Company.
Manufactured in the United States of America

Library of Congress Cataloging in Publication Data

Hinkson, Jim.
   Box lacrosse.

   1. Lacrosse.   I. Title
GV989.H56   796.34'7   74-34016
ISBN 0-8019-6303-6
ISBN 0-8019-6304-4   pbk.

   I am dedicating this book to a man who has had a great influence on my life, Jim Bishop; to a woman who had to put up with me for most of it, my mother; and to my wife Cynndy.

                                                                    J. H.

PREFACE

This book was written from my own personal experiences as a player and as a coach. Hopefully, it will help to produce the better coaches and players we need to upgrade our national game to the status that it so richly merits.

The fast-break, short-pass system will help the great Canadian game of box lacrosse to truly live up to its reputation as the fastest and most exciting game on two feet.

Jim Hinkson

ACKNOWLEDGMENTS

I wish to thank the following people for contributing to this book:

Jim Bishop. Most of my knowledge comes from ten years of association with this man, who is probably one of the greatest coaches and authorities on the game of box lacrosse. He is the most dedicated person I have ever met.

Ron Pither, Bill McTeer, Miss Linda Wright and Joe Krasnaj for their valuable suggestions and advice on preparing this book.

Fred Cooper for all his time and his excellent photos of the Windsor Warlocks.

Ron Duquette for the cover photograph and for the photos on pages 68, 74, 94, 108.

Don Crocker and Pat Baker for their information on goaltending.

Rick Bauer for his information on statistics and his statistical sheets, made up by Ron Pither.

Thom Vann, Pat Healy, Don Crocker, Tom Wright, Mike Burke, Duffy McCarthy and Dave Pillon for doing such a great job of posing for the pictures.

Glen Lotton for his diagram of the lacrosse box.

Miss Ione Paolini for her typing.

Miss A. J. Yorke for her great job as a typist and proofreader. Her help with my first essay was the basis for all this.

My brother Bill, for his enthusiastic encouragement and legal assistance.

J. H.

CONTENTS

INTRODUCTION

Even historians don't know when the first lacrosse stick was made or the first round object propelled through the air. But one thing is certain: nothing in our culture or past is more Canadian than the great Indian game of *baggataway.* Our history shows that hundreds and even thousands of braves participated in playing this early form of field lacrosse. Today, with box lacrosse having taken over from the field game in Canada, lacrosse is now played in every province and territory. In the eastern states of the U.S.A., field lacrosse has continued to be popular, but there has recently been a growing movement toward box lacrosse, with its continuous action appeal for both player and spectator.

Every sport has its day, and right now there is no game growing at the rapid pace of box lacrosse. In less than ten years, it has mushroomed from a local game played in small areas of three Canadian provinces to a major sport played in communities from the interior of British Columbia clear across the country to the rugged terrain of Newfoundland. From a hearty nucleus of some ten thousand players, there are now in excess of a quarter of a million participating, and that figure continues to grow at a rapid rate. It is hoped that a comparable spurt of interest will follow the projected establishment of a professional lacrosse league extending into the United States in the near future.

During the formative years of lacrosse, there has been a great need for a coaching text, and finally we have one. The author, Jim Hinkson, has some outstanding qualities that equip him well to write the first full text on box lacrosse. Though Jimmy didn't start playing lacrosse until well into his teens, he has been a member of several great championship clubs, playing junior lacrosse with the famed Oshawa Green Gaels and then going on to play with Brooklin (Ontario) and Windsor in senior company and the Detroit Olympics and Peterborough Lakers in the professional ranks. Jim has always been a great student of the game and has had to apply himself in an extra special way. This has given him a unique insight into the mechanics and fundamentals, with a particular emphasis on the theory of team play. There is no doubt that the determination and dedication necessary in helping him to expand his own skills have well qualified him to pass on this knowledge to the many young players and coaches across the continent.

At present, Jim heads up his own Physical Education department in an Ontario high school. He is currently active as a player, as well as having coached at both junior and senior levels. There is no question about Jim Hinkson's qualifications to write with authority about the great game of box lacrosse.

Jim Bishop

Executive Vice-President
Detroit Red Wings
(Former Coach
Oshawa Green Gaels,
7 times Canadian Junior
Lacrosse Champions)

1   The Fundamentals of the Fast-Break, Short-Pass System

Box lacrosse is unique in that it contains features of many sports. It has the speed of hockey, the heavy body contact of football and the plays of basketball. The fundamentals that will be dealt with here are specifically related to the fast-break, short-pass system in box lacrosse.

PASSING

In this system the only pass that is stressed is the simple overhand pass. This basic pass is more accurate and quicker to throw than any of the fancy passes. The sidearm, the underhand and the over-the-shoulder passes are certainly more pleasing to the fans, but the chances of not throwing the ball accurately are greater, with the result that the receiver either fumbles or misses the pass. Most fumbles are the fault of the passer, not the receiver.

The Stance

The stance, for a right-handed passer, is similar to that which one would take in throwing a baseball or passing a football (*Figure 1*). The passer should stand with his left side facing the receiver and with his left foot slightly forward, pointing toward the receiver, while the back foot is at close to a ninety-degree angle to the front foot.

Holding the Stick

For the right-handed passer (*Figure 2*), the right hand grasps the stick snugly about halfway up the shaft. The left hand is placed at the butt of the stick, which is again held snugly by the fingers. Be sure both thumbs lie flat along the shaft.

Figure 2

Figure 1

3

The stick should be held to the outside of the body with the butt end below the right shoulder. Beginners have a bad habit of holding the butt of the stick in front of their stomachs. This will throw off their pass. Holding the stick vertically over the shoulder (with the gutted pocket facing the receiver and the butt end of the stick pointing toward the receiver) assures the passer that the ball will go straight ahead somewhere in this vertical plane; then all he has to do is find the level at which to release the ball. This position of the stick helps to ensure a fluid movement rather than a stiff, jerky one.

Figure 3

Throwing Action

Both arms are used in getting power and accuracy in the pass. In throwing the ball, both wrists are snapped in a whip-like motion. The arm of the top hand (right) is extended fully during the follow-through, while the arm of the lower hand (left) remains flexed (*Figure 3*). Many beginners, instead of throwing the ball, try to push it by extending both their arms. This technique should be avoided.

Before the actual pass, the body weight is on the rear foot; as one swings the stick forward, the weight is transferred to the forward foot. This not only gives the passer balance, it helps to put power into his pass. It is also the basis of a good habit, for the player is usually running when he passes and will automatically pass off the foot opposite the stick.

On the follow-through, rotate the hips so that the shoulders end up facing the receiver after the release of the ball. This also adds power to the pass.

The Pass

The only pass recommended is a high outside pass on the stick side of the receiver, *i.e.,* about two feet above the shoulder and one foot outside it. Stress throwing a pass for accuracy at first and not for speed. Many players try to throw the ball too hard and consequently lose their accuracy. A pass is meant to be caught.

Discourage long passes except to players who have breakaways. The possibility of interceptions is too great, and the probability of the receiver catching the long pass is much lower than for short passes.

A passer should never throw a bounce pass, for as the ball comes off the floor, the receiver might miss it because of a dirty bounce or a misjudgment of its angle. Also, the ball coming off the floor has a spin which makes it very difficult to catch.

(*Note:* For this short-pass system the pocket of the stick should not be too deep. This will make it possible to get a pass away more quickly.)

Passing to a Moving Player

The pass stressed in such sports as football and hockey is the "lead" pass, where the passer throws the football or passes the puck in front of the receiver. Lacrosse is the only game in which the pass is thrown behind the receiver rather than in front. In lacrosse, because players play on the opposite side of the floor to which they shoot (*i.e.*, right-hand shots play on the left side of the floor and vice-versa), their sticks will be behind their shoulders as they run down the floor (*Figure 4*). The speed of the pass must be timed with the speed of the receiver so that the ball will end up slightly behind him. The player then catches the ball in the stick-shoulder area, and as soon as he does so, he is in a position to shoot or pass.

Sometimes lead passes are thrown to more advanced players, but this is usually done only when the player has a breakaway.

A ball should never be thrown directly over a moving player's head unless he has a breakaway. This type of pass, called a "suicide" pass, causes

the receiver to turn his head to look for the ball and thus sets him up for a check from his blind side. If the ball carrier is running down the floor behind one of his teammates to whom he wishes to pass, he should cut to the center of the floor and pass to his teammate on an angle rather than dead on. This makes for an easier pass to catch, and the receiver can use his peripheral vision to look for the ball as well as for any opponent who might be in the area.

Figure 4

Figure 5

CATCHING

Although most fumbles are the result of the passer throwing balls astray, many are also the fault of the receiver who errs in not knowing how to catch the ball.

Receiving Action

In receiving, the placement of the hands is usually the same as in the throwing action. The top hand can either slide up the shaft to the throat of the stick to make it easier to catch the ball, or the top hand can remain stationary around the middle of the shaft, whichever feels natural to the receiver. The receiver should hold the stick loosely, mainly with the fingers, in a relaxed grip.

When receiving the pass, let the stick "give" slightly at the moment of contact with the ball (*Figure 5*). This "give," or backward motion of the stick, cushions the force of the ball and is accomplished by relaxing the arm of the upper hand (right). If the receiver doesn't give with the stick, the ball will bounce out of the pocket of the stick. At first the ball may roll out when the stick is dropped back, but eventually it will become natural to know, without looking, how far one can drop the stick back without the ball rolling out. The stick should fall back until the netted portion is parallel to the floor. Now, with the stick back, the receiver is ready to throw the ball. This is the beginning of the fast-break system, the in-and-out rhythm of the ball in the stick.

Major Faults in the Receiving Action

When catching, a beginner some-times has a tendency to reach out in front of his body for the ball. When he does this he acquires the bad habit of "twirling" his stick. This is a motion which consists of turning his stick in-ward, using the wrist of the top hand, to keep the ball from falling out of the pocket.

Another common fault often occurs after the player catches the ball. This is the habit of "cradling" the ball in an effort to keep it in the pocket. It is simply a continuous rocking motion of the stick (up and down), again using the wrist of the top hand, with the lower hand remaining stationary but holding the stick loosely with the fingers so that the shaft can rotate easily. The only time a player should cradle the ball is in the process of taking a check (see Body Fake, page 8).

In both these actions, while the re-ceiver is attempting to keep the ball in the pocket, it is possible for the passer to give his checker a "deke," get into the clear for a very short time for a return pass, then be picked up again by his checker before the receiver can get his stick back to pass.

Receiving the Pass

The most important thing about re-ceiving a pass is to always give the passer a target indicating where you want to receive the ball (see Figure 4, page 5). Sometimes when a player gets a breakaway, it might be better reception strategy for him to hold his stick out in front of his body rather than over his shoulder (*Figure 6*). This way he can catch the lobbing lead pass

Figure 6

Figure 7

more easily than by taking it over his shoulder (see Goaltender as an Offensive Weapon, page 91). Usually, however, passes are taken over the shoulder.

INDIVIDUAL OFFENSE

Here are some moves which can be used in attempting to beat the defensive man. In general, these moves are for a straight one-on-one situation with the offensive man carrying the ball. It is recommended that some of the moves be tried during a game even when a player doesn't have the ball.

In most of these offensive moves, keep the stick between the body and the checker and tucked in close enough to the body so that the ball cannot be knocked loose. An alternative move is to hold the stick out far enough so that the defensive man is unable to reach it (*Figure 7*).

Body Fake

The general idea here is to get the defensive man to commit himself to go one way while the offensive player goes the other way.

The common body fake is an attempt to get the defensive man to move back and forth by faking one way and then the other (*Figure 8*). As the checker starts to commit himself to one of the fakes, the ball carrier goes around him. The ball carrier takes the check on the upper arm (padded) or on the back area (slightly padded). He should not stand erect, as he will be easy to knock down. Instead, he should lean into the check so that it will be harder to knock him down. He absorbs the impact of the check by relaxing his body. He should also relax his hold on the stick, or the ball will be jarred loose. The body is kept between the stick and the checker, with the stick tucked in close enough to the body so that the defensive man cannot hit it. This is the only time a player should cradle a stick so that the ball will not be lost (*Figure 9*; see Catching, page 6).

Figure 8

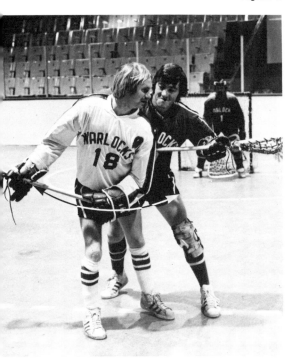

Figure 9

Figure 10

If the offensive man is stopped by the defensive man, a good strategy is for him to expose more of the stick, thus making it so tempting for the checker that he can't resist going after it. As he makes a move to check the stick, it should be pulled around in front of the body so that the offensive man ends up around his checker (*Figures 10-12*).

Figure 12

Figure 11

Figure 13

Another move is the outside fake (*Figure 13*), which is executed by coming straight in on the defensive man and giving him a small step (fake) to the outside, *i.e.,* toward the boards. As the defensive man commits himself to check the ball carrier, the ball carrier pushes off hard with the same foot and takes a large step with the other foot to the inside, *i.e.,* toward the center of the floor. The inside fake is just the reverse of the outside fake, except that as the ball carrier cuts to the outside,

he switches the stick to the outside hand to cradle the ball and prevent the stick from being hit. This time he cuts behind the defensive man to the net.

Stick Fake

The ball carrier fakes an overhand shot or pass by turning his stick inward. This motion is produced by twisting the wrist of the top hand and holding the stick loosely in the fingers of the bottom hand so that it can

11

Figure 14

Figure 15

Figure 16

Figure 17

Figure 18

rotate easily (see Catching, page 6, and Fake Shot, page 30). On such a move a defensive player will usually either go for the stick or tense up. As he goes for the stick, the offensive man tries to get his shoulder and inside foot past the defensive man to the outside and consequently around him (*Figures 14-16*); or as the defensive man tightens up, the ball carrier will use the defender as a screen and shoot either over him (*Figure 17*) or around him (*Figure 18*).

Change of Pace

This is a slowing-down motion by the ball carrier as he approaches the defensive man, then a quick acceleration. Usually the break is to the outside, but if timed correctly it can be an effective move executed to the inside.

Pivot

The pivot is a very good move if executed correctly. The ball carrier pivots to the inside so that when the pivot is completed the player is in position, facing the net, to take a shot. Practice in pivoting both ways helps to make a player more versatile.

For a right-handed man to pivot around his man, he must first fake a drive to the outside to set up his defensive man (*Figure 19*). He then pushes quickly off his left foot (fake foot), while placing his right foot (pivot foot) outside of his opponent's inside foot (*Figure 20*). As he swings his non-pivot foot (left foot) backward, he transfers his body weight to his pivot foot.

Figure 19

Figure 20

14

As he spins around on his pivot foot (on the toes), he tucks his stick in close to his body to shield it from the defensive man and leans his body weight into the stick of his opponent (*Figure 21*). He should continue to roll off the tip of the stick or to the inside of the body,

Figure 21

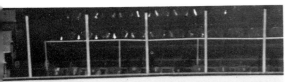

Figure 22

thus ending up around his man (*Figure 22*). As in taking a check, the body is relaxed when leaning into the defensive man's stick. If a player stiffens his body when taking a check or holds his stick too rigid, the ball will be jarred loose from the stick.

INDIVIDUAL DEFENSE

Lacrosse is one of the few games in which a player can become an adept offensive player as well as a defensive player. On offense everybody should be a scoring threat, and when on defense everybody should be a checker.

Figure 23

Checking Strategy

Before even going on the floor, a player should study his opponents to know what their favorite moves are. Most players have one good move for beating a man and seldom vary from this predictable pattern. Here are some questions a player should think about when checking a man: Is he a good long ball shooter? Does he like to work in close to get his shot off? Does he like to beat you to the inside or to the outside?

On the floor, before a player actually comes in contact with the ball carrier, he must get himself mentally prepared. He can probably do this by simply making up his mind that his check is not going to beat him. Next, he must get himself physically "set," with arms and knees flexed ready to make the contact.

Cross-Check

The cross-check is the main method used to stop the ball carrier from scoring. Usually, a left-handed shot will try to pick up a right-handed opponent to check and vice versa. This is so that his stick will be on the same side as his check's stick. He can then interfere with his check's pass or shot.

1. Stance

The stance for cross-checking is very important (*Figure 23*). The feet should be parallel, with one foot slightly ahead of the other. A wide base is necessary, with feet at least shoulder width apart. Weight should be on the balls of the feet and evenly distributed. This affords balance as well as the ability to move laterally. If the weight is on the heels, a player will be caught flat-footed and unable to move laterally quickly enough.

Figure 24

If the weight is on the toes, a player will be easy to knock down.

The body should be in a slightly crouched position, with knees bent, back fairly straight and head up. The arms should be flexed, holding the stick with a tight, firm grip. The hands should be placed fairly wide apart. A player should remember to turn his stick a quarter turn so that he is checking against the grain of the wood. If the stick is not turned, it can become warped or broken from cross-checking.

2. Contact

A good defensive player should always let the opponent make the first move before attempting a cross-check. Don't lunge at the ball carrier. If a checker does not exercise patience and charges the ball carrier, he will over-commit himself (with arms fully extended yet not touching or only slightly touching the opponent) and be off balance, thus making it easy for the ball carrier to go around him (*Figures 24, 25*).

Figure 25

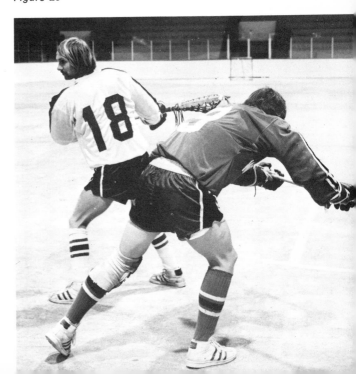

Figure 26

A bad habit to get into is to "back-pedal" in trying to throw off the ball carrier. A defensive man should hold his ground when cross-checking. In this way he will have the stable footing needed for the power of a solid cross-check.

With the arm muscles flexed, wait for the ball carrier to get about a foot and a half away before you "explode." At the moment of the explosion, the checker shoots his arms out, with his whole body weight behind them, coming into solid contact with his opponent. Try to hit the player squarely on the arm pad or on the back (*Figure 26*) so that there is no chance of the stick slipping up over the shoulder. This would result in a high-sticking penalty. A stiff enough check might jar the ball loose from the ball carrier's stick. One of the best times to hit a man is at the exact time when he is shooting, for the jar of the check could throw off his shot.

3. Footwork

The checker should stay low and square to his offensive man, constantly "bugging" his stick or throwing stiff cross-checks. Here, his footwork is very important. He should use the "shuffle," which is a sideways sliding movement of the feet. If he crosses his feet, he is likely to trip himself or throw himself off balance (*Figure 27*).

Figure 27

4. Checking a Larger Player

Sometimes a defensive man ends up checking a ball carrier who is quite large. The favorite move of the big player is usually to overpower his opponent to get into scoring territory. To counteract this move, the defender should play him in one of two ways. 1) As the larger player starts to lean into the stick, back away so that he is now slightly off balance and then, as he concentrates on regaining his balance, knock his stick, jarring the ball loose. 2) Rather than playing the ball carrier head on, play him off center to his stick side (*Figure 28*). This move will force the ball carrier to the outside. As he tries to get past the checker by pulling his stick around his own body, he will leave an exposed area under the arm where the checker can put his stick to push the ball carrier to the boards (*Figure 29*).

Figure 28

Figure 29

Stick Check

The actual stick check is done when double-teaming the ball carrier while on the power-play defense or when "blitzing" the ball carrier on the five-on-five defense. Players can blitz any time when on defense. The crucial factor is the selection of the perfect time to do it. Blitzing occurs when the ball carrier is tied up by his checker and is unable to pass the ball or to shoot; the checker's teammate on the same side of the floor, when he sees the ball carrier in trouble, leaves his check and rushes over to check the ball carrier's stick. The original checker plays the ball carrier as he normally would (checking his body), while his teammate goes for the stick. The checker never goes for the

Figure 30

Figure 31

pocket area of the stick, but either to a spot near the neck of the shaft or to a spot close to the top hand, because in this area the stick moves less and is easier to hit (see Power-Play Defense in the Defensive Zone, page 66).

The major rule in checking is never to go for a ball carrier's stick when cross-checking. If a defensive player tries for his opponent's stick, or in other words, makes the first move, the ball carrier can go around him very easily, because the checker will be off balance. But if the ball carrier does beat his defensive man, all the checker does is wait for the ball carrier to pull back on his stick to shoot. When he does this, the checker simply bangs down or up on his stick, knocking the ball loose (*Figure 30;* see Chasing Drill, page 98).

Body Check

This move is used primarily when the offensive man pushes the checker's stick against his body. Unable to use his stick, but still attempting to prevent the offensive man from going around him, the defensive man resorts to using his upper body (shoulders and chest). If his opponent tries to beat him to his right, the defensive man puts his right shoulder and arm, bent out to the side, into the body of his opponent to block his attempt (*Figure 31*). He uses this move until he has a chance to recover his original cross-checking position.

Figure 32

LOOSE BALLS

The importance of loose balls cannot be stressed enough. When a team has possession of the ball they control the game. Therefore, the more loose balls the team gets, the more chances they will have to score. It would be quite logical to say that games are won and lost on loose balls.

There are three main ways of picking a ball up from the floor.

The Trap-and-Scoop

Here, the player first stops the ball from rolling or bouncing by trapping it under the mesh (*Figure 32*). He then pulls his stick back with a raking motion until the ball comes out from underneath the mesh. As the ball comes out, he pushes his stick forward, scooping the ball into his pocket. This move is accomplished with both hands on the stick. A player should try to shield the ball with his body while picking it up (see Loose Ball Drill, page 98).

Figure 34

Figure 33

The Scoop

This is usually executed on the dead run when there isn't enough time to trap the ball or when the ball is bouncing and doesn't have to be trapped. This pickup involves a shovel-like motion. Again, both hands should be on the stick. Sometimes a player may have to use one hand, in which case he grips the middle of the shaft to snare the ball, while warding off a check with the other arm (*Figure 33*).

The ball should never be scooped directly off the floor with the stick held in front of the body. The stick should be held to the side of the body (*Figure 34*); in this way, if the mouth of the stick jams into the floor, the butt end won't jam into the player's stomach.

Figure 35

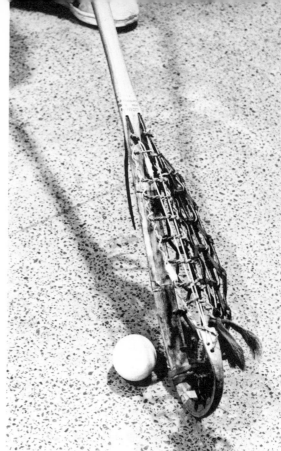

Figure 36

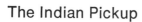

Figure 37

The Indian Pickup

Probably the hardest pickup to execute, this involves the tip of the stick. Hold the stick with one hand (in left hand if a right-handed shot) somewhere between the middle of the shaft and the butt end. Invert the stick (*Figure 35*) and bang the ball off the inside of the wooden guard (*Figure 36*), flicking it into the pocket while turning the stick upright (*Figure 37*). This pickup enables a player to reach into a scramble for a loose ball and pick it up.

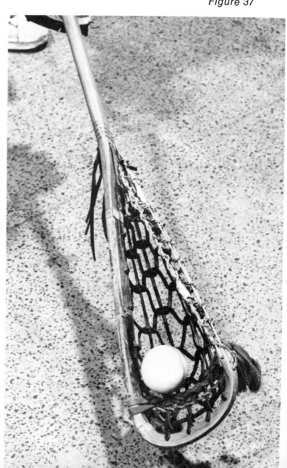

SHOOTING

To win, a team must score more goals than the opposition; thus it is obvious that the shooting aspect of lacrosse is very important. Many players hesitate to shoot in a game because they don't have the necessary confidence in their shot. If a player doesn't shoot, he certainly can't score. A player should work on his shooting in practice so that he will have the confidence he needs in a game.

Many players like to shoot very hard ("bomb" their shots), and although this may intimidate the goalie and make a loud noise when the ball hits the boards, it won't score many goals. As in passing, the first thing to stress in shooting is accuracy. Afterwards the players can start to work on speed.

To become an efficient goal scorer, a player must learn to "pick." In other words, he should never shoot without knowing the spot he is aiming at. An equally bad mistake a player can make is to "telegraph" his shot, or look at the spot he is going to shoot at so that the goalie can anticipate the shot even before the player takes it (*Figure 38*). A player must learn to use his peripheral vision, that is, be able to look at the whole net, yet zero in on one spot.

Figure 38

Figure 39

Figure 40

There are approximately five types of shots used in lacrosse.

The Overhand Shot

The same principles are applicable to the overhand shot that were used in the overhand pass, except that in the shot there is more emphasis on getting the body weight behind the ball (see Passing, page 2). This is accomplished by following through more with the stick and bending more at the waist (*Figure 39*).

A player can shoot long or close-in shots from the overhand position, aiming for the high or low corners of the net. Also, a bounce shot may be taken from this position by placing the ball about a foot in front of the goalie. The bounce shot is probably the most difficult shot for a goalie to stop, especially for a big goalie, as he will have little lateral movement (*Figure 40*). The bounce shot is used for the same reason that the bounce pass is not advised: when the ball comes off the floor the goalie has to readjust his eyes and try to judge the angle of the bounce.

A player should try to master the basic overhand shot first, before attempting any other type of shot.

The Sidearm Shot

This shot involves a baseball-swing motion, with the stick held in a horizontal position and both hands at the end of the stick. The follow-through is accomplished by snapping both wrists (*Figures 41-43*). For best accuracy, this shot should be taken from around the free-throw line.

Figure 41

Figure 42

Figure 43

Figure 44

Figure 45

Figure 46

The Underhand Shot

This shot is similar to a golf swing, with both hands at the butt of the stick. As in the other shots, the follow-through is accomplished by a whip-like motion of the wrists (*Figures 44-46*). It is hard for a goalie to predict where this shot is going, as a player can change the direction of the shot by a slight twist of the wrists.

This shot can also be used very effectively from around the free-throw line. The shot is usually low but can be a very deceptive shot if the ball is made to rise. An underhand bounce shot is an extremely effective offensive weapon.

The Over-the-Shoulder or Backhand Shot

Crossing in front of the net, the player continues his regular shooting motion until he is practically past it. This causes the goalie to hug the post. The player then shoots his stick back over his shoulder for the open side of the net. He does this by turning his stick slightly inward and extending the arm of the top hand out to his side and flexing it (*Figure 47*).

This shot should be mastered in practice before it is applied in a game.

Figure 47

Figure 48

Figure 49

The Fake Shot

The fake shot is usually used close in, but many players will fake a long shot, forcing the goalie to come out to cover the angle (*Figure 48*). They will then quickly change their pace to take a close-in shot behind the goalie, who has now moved out to the crease (*Figure 49*).

Faking is the same motion as twirling the stick. However, the ball carrier must give the impression that he is really going to shoot at one side of the net, and at the moment of the follow-through he must "check" his shot and shoot at the other side. This twirling or checking action is accomplished by using the wrist of the top hand to turn the stick inward, while holding the butt end loosely with the fingers of the other hand so that the stick can rotate easily in one's grip (*Figure 50*;

Figure 50

Figure 51

see Catching, page 6, and Stick Fake, page 11). The fake works very well on a "reflex" goalie.

Players are sometimes told that when shooting they should keep the head of the stick still (*Figure 51*). In other words, there should be no faking at all; but by experimenting, players can establish what is most successful for them individually.

2   The Fast-Break, Short-Pass System

Most lacrosse is played in a free-lance style in which there are not many set plays. In the fast-break system there are set positions for each player in the attacking zone. The players are disciplined to run to these specific areas and then work their plays from there.

The two forwards or wingers are called creasemen. The centerman takes the position of a cornerman (left cornerman if he is a right-handed shot or right cornerman if he is a left-handed shot). One of the defensemen (opposite shot to the centerman) fills in the other cornerman's position, while the second defenseman will position himself a little to the left or right of the center area, again

depending on which shot he is, as the pointman.

BREAK-OUT PATTERN

The fast break can originate from loose balls, from interceptions or from the goaltender. If it begins from the goaltender, there are certain positions the players take in their defensive zone. All five players then break out of their own end as a unit, the whole idea of the fast-break system being to catch an opponent behind the play.

Even before the players receive the ball from the goalie they must position

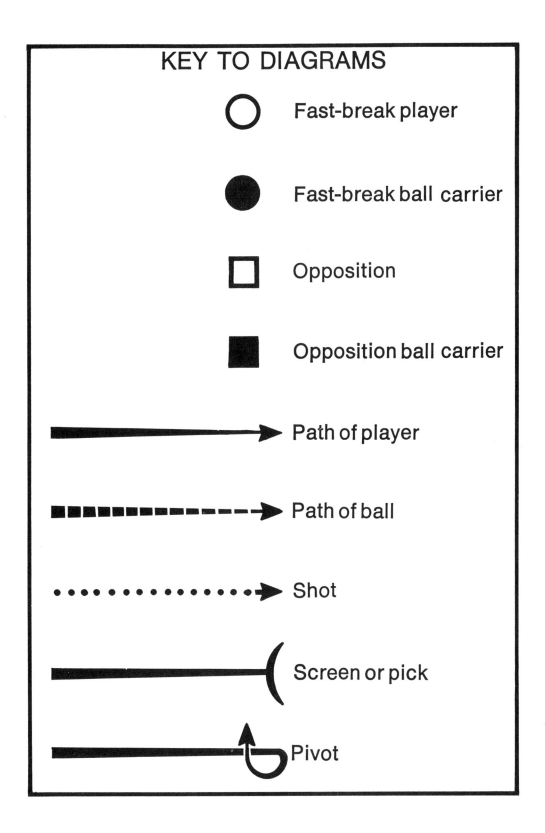

KEY TO DIAGRAMS

○   Fast-break player

●   Fast-break ball carrier

□   Opposition

■   Opposition ball carrier

⟶   Path of player

⇢   Path of ball

⋯▶   Shot

⊢   Screen or pick

↱   Pivot

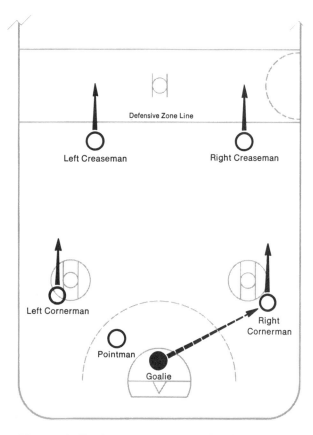

Diagram 1   Break-out Pattern for Fast Break

and therefore should be expecting the pass. The pass from the goalie triggers every player to break out as fast as he can into the attacking zone. There should be only one or two short passes all the way down the floor. This reduces the chances of a fumble or an interception.

If the situation arises where the goalie can throw a long pass to one of his "open" creasemen, he should do so. The creaseman can then run the ball deep into the offensive zone, looking back (if he is now being checked) for his cornerman and pointman breaking into the clear for a pass.

SET POSITIONS

The creasemen plant themselves on the edge of the crease in scoring territory (Diagram 2). They do not break across in front of the net, but remain stationary. The cornermen break down behind their respective creasemen, making sure in each case that the distance between cornerman and creaseman is large enough so that one defensive player won't be able to check both at once. The pointman takes his position to the right or left of the center area.

In the fast-break system the positions are interchangeable, but only after the players have learned their specific positions. For example, if a cornerman ends up down the floor ahead of a creaseman, he simply takes the creaseman's position.

ODD-MAN SITUATIONS OFFENSIVELY

The objective of the fast-break system is to get the ball into the attacking zone as quickly as a team can, creating an odd-man situation. An odd-man situation occurs when an offensive team has one

themselves in their designated areas (Diagram 1). The two cornermen position themselves wide around the two end zone face-off circles to avoid a congestion of players in the center area and the possibility of an interception. The pointman stands near his goalie's crease. The two creasemen place themselves at the defensive zone line until they know they have possession, and then they will break in a straight line to the edge of the opposing goalie's crease.

In starting the fast break, the goalie throws a short pass to either the pointman or the cornerman. The cornerman opposite the pointman (weak-side cornerman) is the main target for the goalie more player in the attacking zone than its opposition. There are set responsibilities for each player in the fast-break system. These will be shown through the following plays.

The Two-on-One

The two-on-one play usually consists of two creasemen breaking in on one defenseman. The creasemen must break quickly up the floor and end up close to the goaltender's crease, so that when they do get the pass they will be a scoring threat. What is stressed here offensively is that the ball carrier draws the defenseman over to him and then passes to the player in the open. A player should never pass a ball when taking a check. A cross-check could easily throw the pass off. As a player fades back to avoid the cross-check, he is pulling the defenseman out of the play, giving his teammate more time and room to fake his shot on the goalie once he receives the pass.

The Three-on-Two

The fast break occurs many times from the face-off (see Face-offs, page 75). Again, hitting the player in the clear is stressed (*Diagram 3*). When a defenseman rushes out to check the centerman,

Diagram 2   Set Positions for the Fast-break System

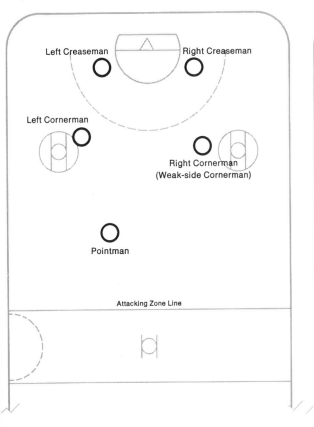

Left Creaseman   Right Creaseman

Left Cornerman

Right Cornerman
(Weak-side Cornerman)

Pointman

Attacking Zone Line

Diagram 3   Three-on-Two Fast Break

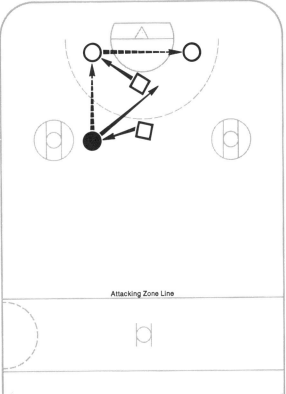

Attacking Zone Line

he passes off to a creaseman in the clear, who will take a shot on net or, if the other defensive player comes over to check him, will pass to the other creaseman. The centerman tries to draw a checker, but if the two defensive men sag back and stay with the two creasemen, he should move in and shoot. Sometimes a centerman will pass the ball to one creaseman and set a "screen" for the other creaseman, who will in turn get the pass (see Screens, page 42).

If the three-on-two fast break originates from the defensive zone, the creasemen should break directly to the crease, looking for the occasional pass.

Diagram 4   Four-on-Three Fast Break

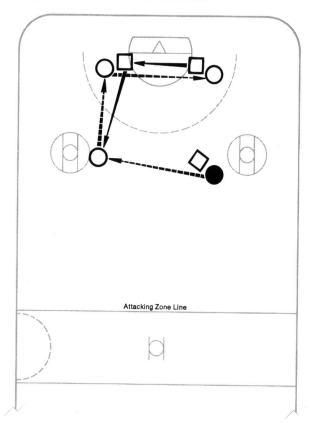

Attacking Zone Line

The Four-on-Three

This is the most common situation in lacrosse and is the "bread and butter" play of the fast-break system (*Diagram 4*).

Here, one of the defensemen, opposite shot to the centerman, fills in the other cornerman's position. The cornerman with the ball tries to draw the front defensive man. If he succeeds, he then passes to the other cornerman, who has two options. He can either take a clear shot on net or, if a defensive man rushes out at him, back off and lob a pass to the open creaseman. If a defensive man rushes across to check this creaseman, he should pass over to the opposite creaseman.

The Five-on-Four

The pointman is important in this play, because if he doesn't outrun the last opponent up the floor, the play will not work (*Diagram 5*). Usually the cornerman on the side opposite to the pointman (weak-side cornerman) ends up with the ball in the attacking zone; he then passes it to the creaseman on his side of the floor. The pass is given to the creaseman so that the defensive players will have a harder time keeping track of their opponents and the ball at the same time.

As the defensive men look back for the ball, the cornerman on the same side as the pointman breaks in front of his checker, looking for the pass. If his checker doesn't stay with him, he will get the pass from the creaseman. If his checker does stay with him, he won't get the pass but will leave an open area for the pointman to step into; the pointman will, in turn, get the pass from the creaseman.

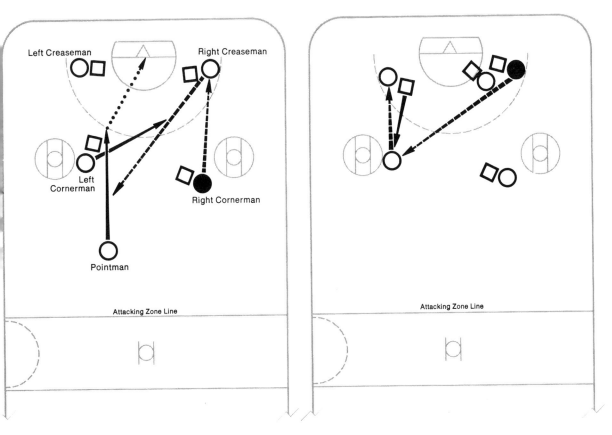

Diagram 5 Five-on-Four Play to Pointman

Diagram 6 Five-on-Four Play to Creaseman

If the pointman finds he can't get his shot away because one of the defensive players has rushed out to check him, he will give a short pass to the open creaseman (*Diagram 6*). The cornerman who was being checked as he broke through the center can set a screen for the creaseman with the ball, so that in case he can't get the pass to the pointman he can use the screen.

3 Team Offense

OFFENSIVE PLAYS

There are some basic plays for the five-on-five offense in the fast-break system which, if executed properly, will add much effectiveness to the attack. These are the give-and-go, the screen, the pick-and-roll and the pivot-screen.

The Give-and-Go

When a player passes the ball to a teammate, he has the option of cutting in front of or behind the defensive man who is checking him. To execute the inside give-and-go, the player, after throwing the ball, must relax so that his checker relaxes slightly. When the defensive man lets up on his checking, the former ball carrier fakes to the outside and then breaks to the inside for the return pass (*Diagram 7*). He should break straight across the floor so that on receiving the pass he will cross in front of the net, giving himself a good angle to

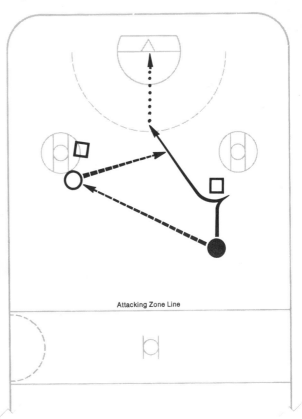

Diagram 7   The Inside Give-and-Go

Attacking Zone Line

shoot at the goal. Many players, after breaking in front of their checker, will break down the side rather than straight across, but this will cut down their shooting angle. The speed of the return pass and the quickness of the breaker must combine to make this a successful play.

If the defensive man plays out far enough from the goal area, the offensive man can cut behind him or to the outside of him by using the change of pace move or an inside fake (*Diagram 8*; see Individual Offense, page 8). If this move is not executed quickly enough and the pass not thrown properly, there is the possibility of an interception by this defensive man, who will now be between the passer and the receiver.

The Screen

A screen is just an interference for a teammate's checker. To work properly, the screen must be set inconspicuously. Therefore, it is not up to the player setting the screen to make it work, but to the teammate being screened. The screening player tries to set the screen in the general area of the teammate whom he is screening (*Diagram 9*). The teammate being screened must then try to work his opponent into the screen. The teammate must fake outside, then go around his screen, making sure he touches his screen's shoulder. As his teammate passes him, the screening player pivots. He holds his stick in such

Diagram 8 The Outside Give-and-Go

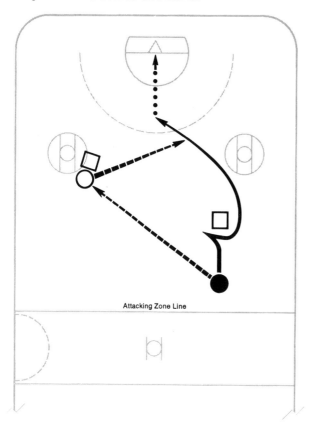

Diagram 9 The Screen

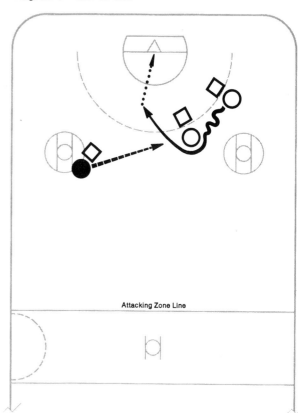

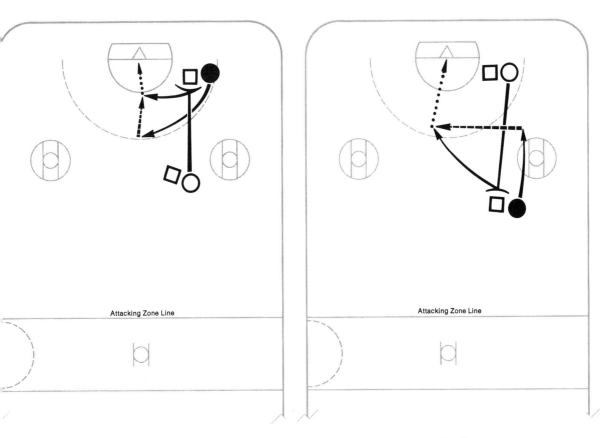

Diagram 10   Pick-and-Roll by Cornerman

Diagram 11   Pick-and-Roll by Creaseman

a manner (in a horizontal position at waist level) that it will interfere with the progress of his defensive man, who has "switched" in an effort to check the screening player's teammate (see Switch, page 56).

A "pick" is set in the same way as a screen except that it is set for a ball carrier.

The Pick-and-Roll

This is a play perfected for lacrosse by the Peterborough Lakers and is a deceiving play used in counteracting the switch (*Diagram 10*; see Team Defense,

page 56). Here the teammate who sets a conspicuous pick for the ball carrier waits for the defensive man to call "switch," and while they are in the process of switching, he breaks or rolls toward the net for the quick pass from the ball carrier. This teammate will end up on the inside position and therefore closer to the net than the defensive man he blocked out. All he needs then is a step ahead of his defensive man to get the pass and score. Most times, the defensive man guarding this player will relax, as he thinks the play is over. This play can be executed when either the creaseman (see Diagram 10) or the cornerman has the ball (*Diagram 11*).

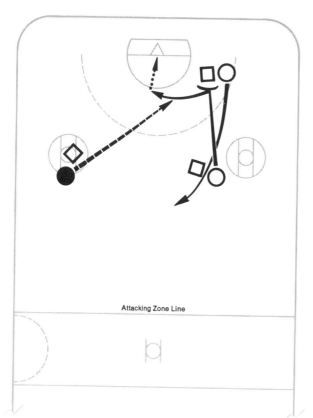

Diagram 12   The Screen-and-Roll

The Pivot-Screen

This is performed when the ball is on the other side of the floor. The cornerman sets a screen for the creaseman on his side. As the creaseman starts to come off the screen, the cornerman pivots beside his checker, while still screening out the creaseman's checker (*Diagram 13*). The ball carrier has two options. He can pass to the pivoting cornerman if he is in the clear, or he can pass to the creaseman coming off the screen.

Diagram 13   The Pivot-Screen

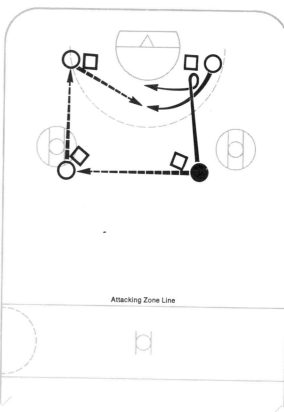

The "screen-and-roll" is executed when the ball is on the other side of the floor. A player will set a so-called screen for a teammate on his own side of the floor. When the teammate cuts around the screen and the defensive man calls the switch, the player who set the screen will cut or roll toward the net for the pass (*Diagram 12;* see Switch, page 56).

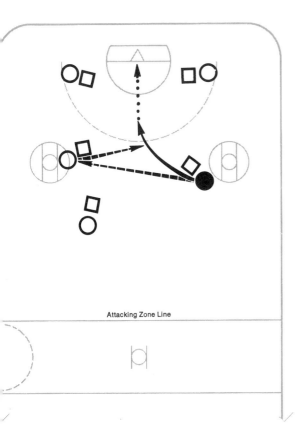

Attacking Zone Line

Diagram 14   Five-on-Five Offense —
Return Pass

BEATING THE DEFENSE

Beating the Man-to-Man Defense

Most of the game is played in the five-on-five situation, and therefore much time should be spent on these time-precision plays.

On offense, players should throw short, quick passes — from one side of the floor to the other and not from the middle of the floor. In this way there is less chance of interceptions. Players should break from their own side, but they don't have to break from the designated area they occupy during the five-on-four situation. When players break across in front of the net, they should run completely through the center rather than stop halfway across. Stopping will create a traffic jam in front of the goal and will obstruct their own teammates from breaking through.

Ball-hogs are unwanted in this type of system, as the opposing team is given a chance to get set by the player hanging on to the ball too long. Passing the ball and constant movement by the players are essential. This activity forces the defensive players to look around to see where the ball is; when they do this, the offensive players will break.

In all these plays (*Diagrams 14-18*) it is assumed that the weak-side cornerman has the ball, but this is just for demonstration purposes. During a game the play can start from any player. The ball carrier usually initiates the play. As soon as the weak-side cornerman passes the ball he has a choice of five set plays:

1) After the pass, he can break for a return pass (*Diagram 14*; see Give-and-Go, page 41).

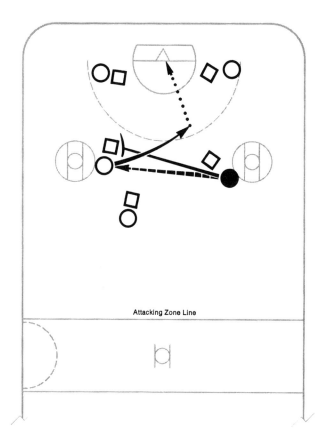

3) He can pass the ball to the other cornerman, who passes it to the creaseman on his own side. The weak-side cornerman then sets a screen or a screen-and-roll for the creaseman on his side of the floor, with the pass going to the cornerman or the creaseman, depending on who is in the clear (*Diagram 16*; see Screen, page 42, and Pick-and-Roll, page 43).

Diagram 15   Five-on-Five Offense — Pick

Diagram 16   Five-on-Five Offense —
Screen or Screen-and-Roll

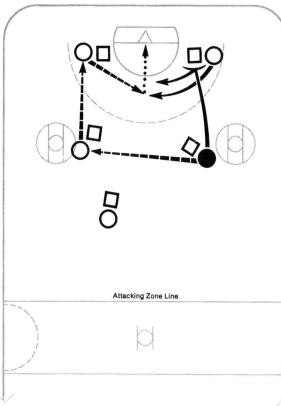

2) If, after the pass, he is too well covered, he can continue on through and set up a pick or a pick-and-roll for the player he just passed to (*Diagram 15*; see Screen, page 42, and Pick-and-Roll, page 43).

4) A double-screen play is used when the weak-side cornerman passes to his creaseman, who passes to the other creaseman coming off a screen set by the opposite cornerman. The weak-side cornerman, in turn, sets a screen for his creaseman, who will receive the return pass from the other creaseman for the shot on net (*Diagram 17*).

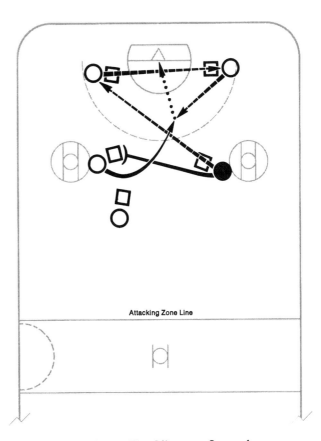

Diagram 18   Five-on-Five Offense — Screen for any Player on Opposite Side

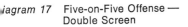

Diagram 17   Five-on-Five Offense — Double Screen

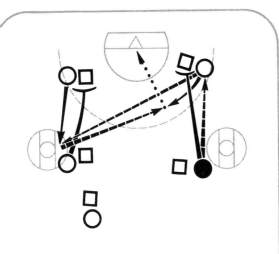

5) After the pass, the weak-side cornerman can set up a screen for a teammate on the opposite side of the floor (other than the ball carrier). This maneuver will trigger the creaseman with the ball to pass it back across to the other creaseman so that he will be in the correct position to give an outside pass to the cornerman coming off the screen (*Diagram 18*).

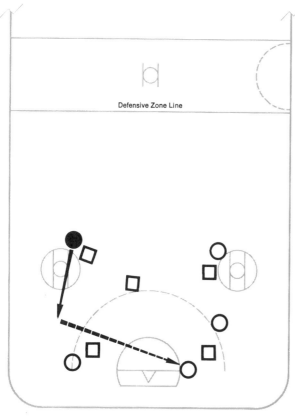

Diagram 19   Beating on One-plus-Four Defense
(behind net)

Diagram 20   Beating the One-plus-Four Defense
(overload)

Beating the Two-One-Two Zone Defense

There are several good ways to beat this defense. Either fast-break out of the defensive zone so that the defensive team doesn't have time to set up the zone defense; or, if they do get a chance to set up this defense, just set up the lines as power-play units, with the shooters on the corners and on the point. The players work as a power-play unit by sending the ball quickly around the outside and passing to the man in the clear. Another way of beating the zone defense is to send two players, one after the other, through the middle and pass to the second man through.

Beating the One-plus-Four Defense

This defense is fairly new to lacrosse, and it would be better to read the section on Defense (pages 57-59) before attempting to read this section.

Many teams beat this defense by having the ball carrier take the ball behind the net so that the defensive players will have to turn their backs slightly on their opponents (*Diagram 19*). When they do this, the offensive players will break down the middle for the pass and the shot. Some teams overload one side instead (*Diagram 20*). One offensive player will place himself in front of the net, and another player will position himself beside the defensive creaseman. There are now two options for the ball carrier: 1) If the defensive creaseman goes to check the player out in front, the ball will be passed to his teammate on the crease.

2) If the defensive creaseman goes to check the offensive creaseman, his teammate out in front of the net will get the pass.

LINE CHANGES

The whole idea of the fast-break system is to keep throwing out fresh running lines to keep up a blistering pace and eventually wear down the opposition. This is why line changes are a part of the offense. How many times in a game has a team been called for too many players on the floor or been caught with not enough players on the floor? Since the play is moving so quickly in this type of system, it is even more important that the players know how to change.

To start with, line changes occur only when the team has possession of the ball. It would be disastrous if a player came off the floor when on defense. Next, each player on the bench must know for whom he is changing (*e.g.*, right cornermen must change only with right cornermen) and who is changing for him. Then, if there is a substitution for one of the players or an injury occurs, he will know who is taking the player's place and with whom to change. The line to go on the floor next should sit together at the door closest to the opposition's net and be ready to go well in advance. Naturally, the line coming off the floor enters through the door closest to their own goal.

Just as in line changes, certain players are designated for the power play and man short. If a player is on the floor at

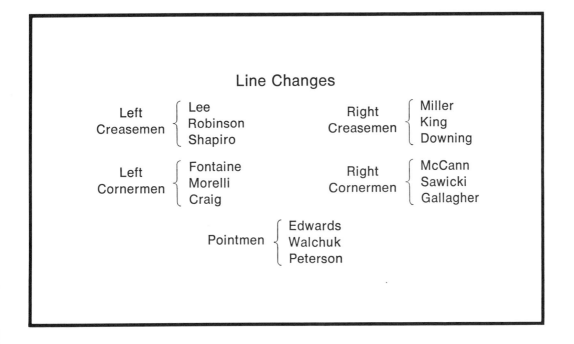

Line Changes

Left Creasemen { Lee, Robinson, Shapiro

Right Creasemen { Miller, King, Downing

Left Cornermen { Fontaine, Morelli, Craig

Right Cornermen { McCann, Sawicki, Gallagher

Pointmen { Edwards, Walchuk, Peterson

the time of a penalty and is not designated for either, he should come off the floor automatically, provided his team has possession of the ball.

On-the-Fly Play

This play is used during line changes when the situation is perfect, *i.e.,* when the weak-side cornerman is opposite the players' bench. All the players go off the floor as a normal line change, except the weak-side cornerman, who runs the ball up the side of the floor into the attacking zone (*Diagram 21*). The four fresh players come on the floor and stay close to the boards opposite this cornerman. Then three of the players cut through the middle all at once, yelling and looking for a pass. Hopefully, there will be some confusion as to which defensive man will check which offensive player. The trailer — the fourth man, who is a shooter — has delayed his break and now cuts through the middle, hopefully unchecked, for the pass and shot.

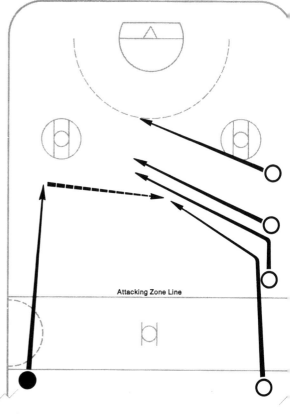

Diagram 21   On-the-Fly Play

Special Units

Man Short #1

Sawicki	Edwards
King	Morelli

Man Short #2

Gallagher	Peterson
McCann	Fontaine

Power Play #1

Lee	Miller
Fontaine	McCann

Morelli

Power Play #2

Robinson	Sawicki
Craig	King

Edwards

4   Team Defense

An aggressive man-to-man defense and the one-plus-four defense complement the fast-break system, as both defenses keep the offensive team moving and busy. First, how to deal with an odd-man situation while on defense will be dealt with.

PLAYING THE ODD-MAN SITUATION DEFENSIVELY

Two-on-One

The lone defensive player can attempt to intercept a pass, force a bad play or simply stall the creasemen from making a play until he gets help. The stick is used here mainly to try to interfere with or delay the play or to intercept a pass. It is important not to get drawn out of position by overrushing the ball carrier. The defensive player should try to stay in the middle area.

Three-on-Two

Here, the defensive players try to force the offensive players to make mistakes. The defensive players play in tandem, with the front man usually charging out to check the ball carrier while his team-mate positions himself between the other two offensive players (*Diagram 22*). Charging means that the defensive man rushes out to the ball carrier, stops about a foot and a half away from him and plants himself to cross-check. The defensive man should try not to get "sucked out" of the play. When a pass is thrown to one of these other two offensive players, the back defensive man will charge the new ball carrier while his teammate positions himself between the old ball carrier and the other player, ready to react to either one of them if a pass is thrown.

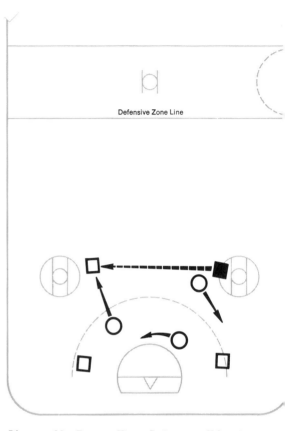

Diagram 23 Four-on-Three Defense — Triangle

Diagram 22 Tandem Defense — Three-on-Two

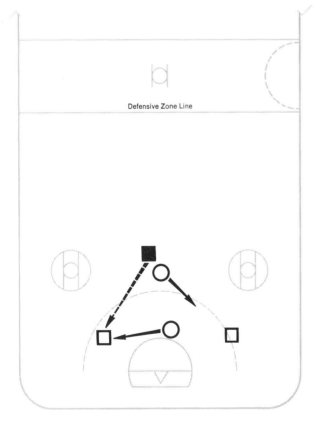

Stick checking is more effective than cross-checking, unless one is certain that he can "hit" the ball carrier with a check stiff enough to throw off his pass. Supportive chatter between the two defensive men is recommended.

Four-on-Three

The same idea is used here as in the tandem defense, except that the three players form a triangular defense. The important thing here is rotation (*Diagram 23*).

Five-on-Four

The players form a "box" defense, in which there must be quick reaction and rotation to prevent the offensive team from getting a good shot on net.

MAN-TO-MAN DEFENSE

The objective of the defense is to stop the opposition from scoring; therefore, when the team loses possession of the ball, the five former offensive players must make a mental commitment to make a defensive reaction back to their defensive zone line. They should run directly over this line and then turn around to face their opponents, each yelling out his check's number. It is amazing how many times players miss their checks in a game. The coach should appoint a defensive captain to make sure everyone has a check, as everyone is a defenseman while the team is on defense.

Checking the Ball Carrier

The player checking the ball carrier should remember not to back in too far. He could either screen the goalie or let the ball carrier into the scoring area. He should harass the ball carrier all the time, either by tapping his stick or by continually cross-checking him. In this way he might make him take a bad shot or throw a bad pass.

Checking the Non-Ball-Carrier

While one player is checking the ball carrier, his teammates should be floating off their men, ready to support this checker in case the ball carrier beats him or in case there is a chance for a blitz (*Diagram 24;* see Stick Checking, page 20).

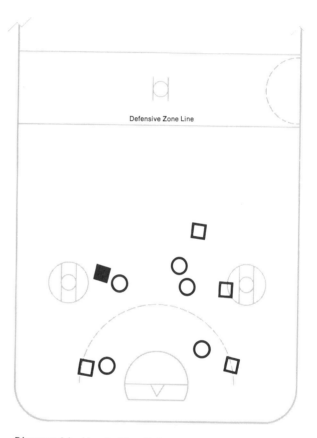

Defensive Zone Line

Diagram 24 Man-to-Man Defense

How a defensive man checks his non-ball-carrier opponent depends upon his man. If his check is a good goal scorer, the defensive man can either pick him up early to make sure he doesn't get the ball at all or play him very close while he is in the defensive zone. If his check isn't a good ball handler or a good goal scorer, the defensive man can probably take a slightly larger risk and play him a little more loosely. In any case, the defensive player must be ready to give his check a small "rap" when he starts to break. This will slow him down or knock him off balance.

Continuous chatter is important on defense. The players can give reassurance to their teammate checking the ball carrier, and the exchange ensures that everyone stays in the game mentally.

Every defensive player should know where the ball is and where his check is at all times. By staying open to the ball, a player can use his peripheral vision to keep an eye on the ball while watching his check at the same time. A player should never turn his back on the ball nor, especially, on his check. Another method of keeping tabs on a check while trying to locate the ball is for a player to put his stick over his check's stick. When his check breaks, he'll know by the movement of his stick.

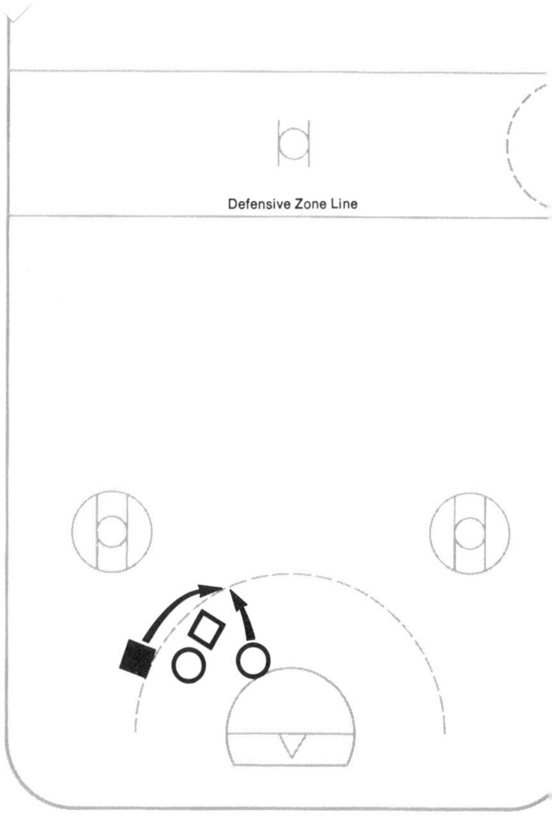

Diagram 25   The Switch

The Switch

The switch is used to counteract the screen and the pick. A switch occurs when a defensive player picks up an offensive man other than the one he is checking (Diagram 25). If the defensive man who is not checking the ball carrier sees that his check is setting a pick, he should first try to push his man out of the play, or his teammate should try to slide through the pick to stay with his man. The man not checking the ball carrier should only call a switch as a last resort. He calls the switch usually because his teammate is being screened out of the play. On calling the switch, the deep man must

move right out on his new check so that this man won't have any room or time to shoot at the net. If a gap occurs between the two men, the ball carrier will certainly shoot.

Stealing the Ball

When a defensive man tries to steal the ball, he must anticipate the pass. Usually the ball is stolen on careless or long passes. The defensive man can take more chances when he is farther away from the goal, because if he fails on his steal he can get defensive help from his teammates.

Pressing Defense

When a team is being continually beaten down the floor by a long pass to a breaking player, the team should combat this by forechecking in their offensive zone. The man nearest the ball carrier will try to stop him from throwing the long pass. This pressing type of defense can also force the opposition team into throwing bad passes.

ONE-PLUS-FOUR DEFENSE

This type of defense can be used by a team if it runs into another team which has good long ball shooters who are physically big. This defense can work for or against a team, depending upon the chasers. If a team is sufficiently aggressive, with a chaser right out on the ball carrier, it may stop the offensive team from even getting a shot on net in the thirty-second time limit, with the result of a "turn-over." If the team is not aggressive, it will give the offensive team the time it needs to pass the ball around and set up plays for a shot on net.

Basic Setup

On setting up the one-plus-four, the team positions itself in a two-one-two zone defense first. The team stays in this position until the ball carrier takes the ball down the side boards or passes to a man on the side. The defensive team doesn't go automatically into the one-plus-four, because it has been found that as the front man goes out to chase the ball carrier in the middle of the floor, he will probably pass off to one of the cornermen. The offensive pointman and

cornermen might pass the ball back and forth, tiring out the front chasers in the one-plus-four.

Ball down the Center

As the ball carrier comes down the middle of the floor, the four men on the corners will play their men fairly close at the beginning to discourage any passes. They will thereby absorb some of the thirty seconds while the defensive man in the center of the zone will move up to the front to check the ball carrier (*Diagram 26*). When this man starts to check

Diagram 26 One-plus-Four Defense — Ball down the Center

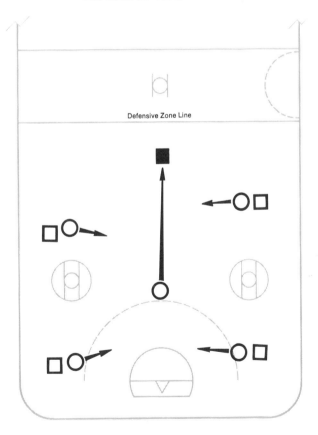

the ball carrier, the other four defensive players start to float off their checks.

Ball to the Side

Once the pass is made to the side, the defensive player closest to the ball carrier will react out to him and start checking him (*Diagram 27*). He should check him with the intention of simply harassing him, to prevent his throwing a good pass. A problem occurs here, because lacrosse players are conditioned to wait for their checks to come to them on defense. In this defense, however, the defensive player must be the aggressor

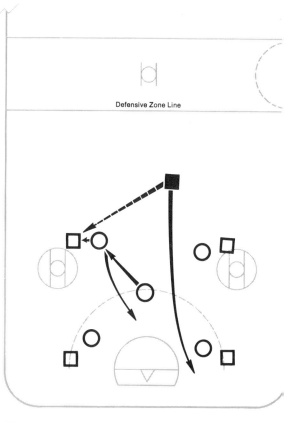

Diagram 28   One-plus-Four Defense —
Man through the Center

Diagram 27   One-plus-Four Defense —
Ball to the Side

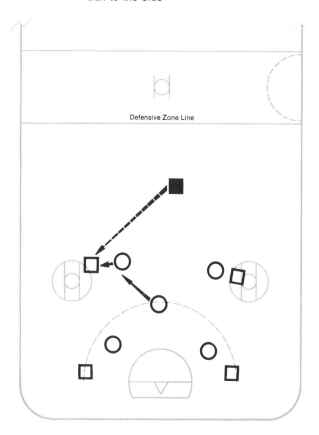

and rush out to the ball carrier, but not to such an extent that he will over-commit himself. He must learn to maintain his basic defensive stance while still annoying the ball carrier.

Here, the main objective for the other defensive players is to try to intercept the pass thrown by the harassed passer. They should be ready to anticipate the pass coming to the offensive man nearest their area.

Man through the Center

If the ball carrier in the middle of the floor passes off to the side, the defensive man closest to the ball carrier will start to check him, and the defensive man in the center of the zone will fill in the area vacated by the chaser. If the offensive man who has just passed the ball cuts through the center, the defensive man who filled in the vacated area will float back and follow this man down the center until he is no longer a threat (*Diagram 28*). If this offensive man goes to one side of the floor to overload it, the defensive man in the center must be alert to intercept any passes intended for this offensive man or for any other offensive player (*Diagram 29*).

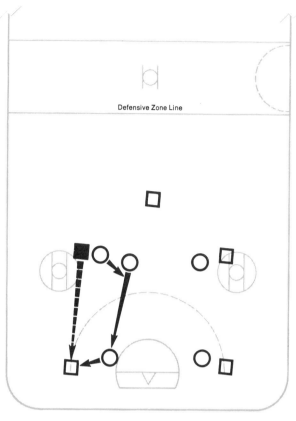

Diagram 30   One-plus-Four Defense —
Ball to the Creaseman

Diagram 29   One-plus-Four Defense —
Playing the Overload

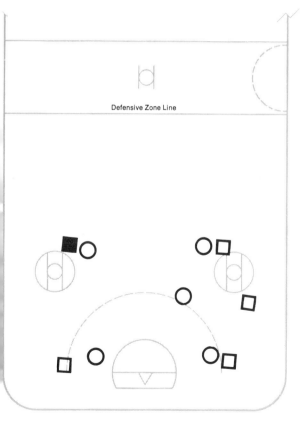

Ball to the Creaseman

If the ball is passed from a cornerman to a creaseman on the same side, the defensive man in this area rushes out and starts checking him, while the defensive man who was backing the other chaser fills in for this one (*Diagram 30*).

5 The Power Play

POWER PLAY WITH POINTMAN

The pointman is the key to making the power play work. He can either hinder it by moving the ball too slowly or make it very effective by moving the ball quickly. Besides being a quick, accurate passer, he must be an especially good shooter. He must shoot intermittently so that he remains a threat; he has to be a scoring threat in order to keep most of the attention of the two front defensive men. Having the ability to throw a backhand pass will make this pointman all the more effective in getting the ball to his cornermen.

The cornermen are usually the main shooters and likewise must have the ability to catch and shoot the ball quickly. The creasemen should be excellent goal scorers close in. They should also be good at retrieving loose balls off the boards and off the goalie. They shouldn't be afraid to go after a ball in the corner or take a hit in front of the net.

The positions of the players on the power play are the same as the fast-break positions, except that the point-man plays exactly on the point rather than to one side or the other of center. The creasemen hold their positions at all times. The cornermen are usually in an

Figure 52

area where they are always a scoring threat so that they keep the attention of the defensive players (*Figure 52*).

If the pointman gets the attention of the two front defensive men, his objective is then to try to set up one of his offensive cornermen (*Diagram 31*). As the pointman passes to his left cornerman, he moves over slightly in that direction. The reason for this is that when the pointman receives the return pass, the defensive cornerman on his right must commit himself to check the pointman to stop him from scoring. As this defensive cornerman rushes to him, the pointman then passes to the right offensive cornerman, who is now in the clear. The pointman can move the ball faster here if he has the ability to throw a backhand pass.

The cornerman, on receiving the ball, has two options: he can either shoot or, if the defensive creaseman rushes out to check him, he can fade back and pass

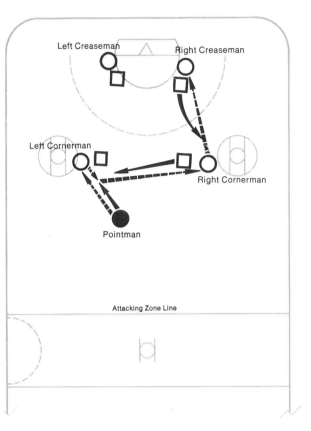

Left Creaseman   Right Creaseman

Left Cornerman

Right Cornerman

Pointman

Attacking Zone Line

Diagram 31   Power Play with Pointman

the ball to the right offensive creaseman. When this creaseman receives the ball, he has three options: 1) if there is no opening he can check his shot and pass the ball back out to the cornerman; 2) if there is an opening, he can take a step out in front of the net for a shot (*Figure 53*), planting himself so that the defensive man has a hard time moving him; 3) if the opposite defensive creaseman rushes

Figure 53

toward him, he can pass to the left offensive creaseman, who will now be in the clear for a shot on net (*Figure 54*).

On the power play, the ball should always travel around the outside. If passed through the center, there is always a chance of an interception.

POWER PLAY WITH CENTERMAN

This is the same type of setup as the ordinary power play, except that the pointman now plays in the center (*Diagram 32*). This player in the center should be fairly big and strong so that he can take the rough going. The cornermen "feed" the creasemen, who in turn, give the ball to the player in the center as quickly as possible. His options are: 1) taking a shot on net, 2) passing back to a creaseman whose check rushes him or 3) passing back to one of the cornermen.

POWER-PLAY DEFENSE

The Press

Because of the ten-second rule, the power-play defense tries to press the

Figure 54

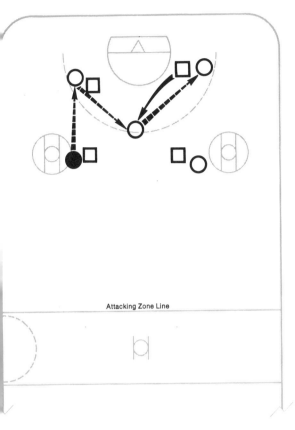

Diagram 32   Power Play with Centerman

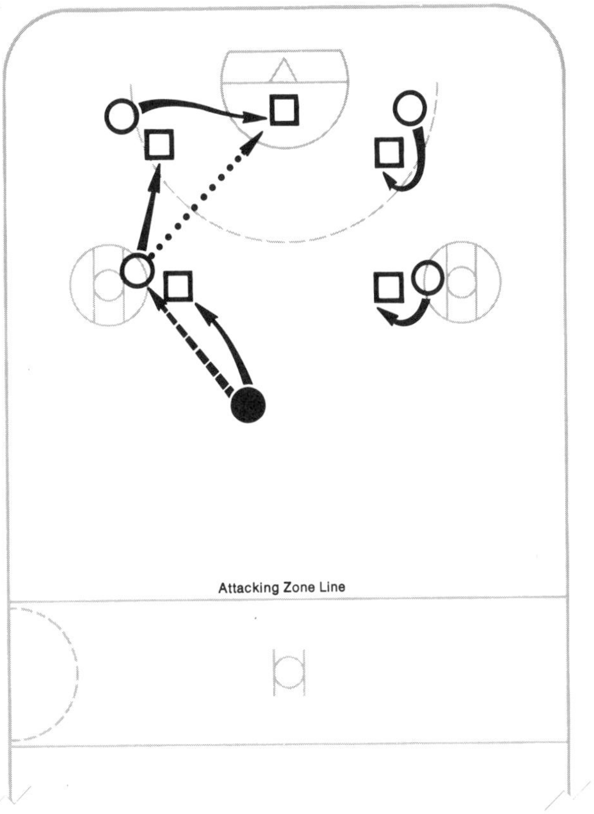

Diagram 33   Power Play — Five-man Press

man-short players in their own defensive zone, so that they will either throw the ball away or use up the ten seconds in trying to get the ball into their attacking zone.

1. The Five-Man Press

In this press, one man will end up checking the goalie. Once the shot has been taken, each offensive player will pick up the opponent closest to him, usually a man who has been designated (*Diagram 33*). If one of the offensive cornermen is the shooter, the pointman

will pick up his defensive cornerman breaking down the floor. Meanwhile, the shooter will pick up the defensive creaseman, leaving the goalie for the offensive creaseman to check. If the pointman ends up shooting, usually the offensive cornerman will check the defensive cornerman when they break down the floor, while the pointman checks the goalie. Every player must stay with his check wherever he goes so that he cannot get the pass. If the goaltender makes the stop and is able to retain the ball, usually one of the creasemen, depending on which cornerman took the shot, will interfere with the goaltender. He does this by waving his stick in front of the goalie's so that the goalie won't be able to throw a perfect pass should one of his teammates end up in the clear.

2. The Four-Man Press

This press is usually used if a team's man-short players consistently get in the clear for the pass and possibly a breakaway. The four men still press their checks, but the pointman reacts back as a safety. Although this will leave the goalie open to throw a good pass, it will cut down on breakaways. If an offensive man beats his checker and gets in the

clear to receive a pass, the safety man will help the defensive man who was beaten, by backing him up.

Power-Play Defense in the Defensive Zone

The power-play players are usually the key players; thus, instead of letting these men tire themselves out trying to get the ball back, fresh players should be sent out whose specific purpose is to retrieve the ball. The fresh players may be five of the better defensive players. These players, as soon as they get possession of the ball, come right off the floor. If a team uses the two-power-play system, then the first power play can chase until they get the ball back, and if they become tired in doing so, then the second power play goes on offensively.

Each player picks up one of the opposition players and sticks to him like glue. The player who positioned himself in the center becomes a chaser, double-teaming the ball wherever it goes (*Diagram 34*). When the ball carrier is double-teamed (see Stick-Checking, page 20), the two players will try to corner him on the boards or force him over their defensive zone line (*Figure 55*).

In this double-team play, one player checks the ball carrier's body while the other player checks his stick (*Figure 56*). It is important that the other players stay close to their checks, because if the ball carrier has no one to whom to pass, he will either be checked into the boards, be pushed over the defensive zone line or panic and throw the ball away.

After the team regains possession of the ball, the original power-play players (or the second power-play players, depending on which system the team uses) come back on to the floor.

Diagram 34   Power Play Defense in Defensive Zone

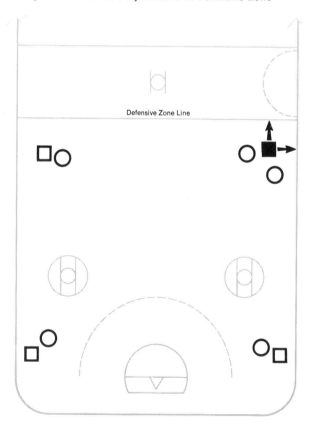

Defensive Zone Line

Figure 55

Figure 55   Figure 56

6 Man-Short Play

MAN-SHORT DEFENSE

Box Defense

This consists of four men forming a box-type defense. Two players are on the crease while two are on the corners. Usually the two players on the corners, or at the front, have their sticks facing into the box to pick off any passes going through the center and to interfere with the pointman's shot. But if the offensive pointman is not a very good shooter, the two front men can switch sides. This will make it easier for them to interfere with the offensive cornermen's shots and will put them in a better position to intercept passes from the pointman to the cornermen.

There are two ways of playing the box, and each team can experiment to find out which one works better for them. In the first situation, the men on the man short should never stay stationary (*Diagram 35*). They should be rotating one

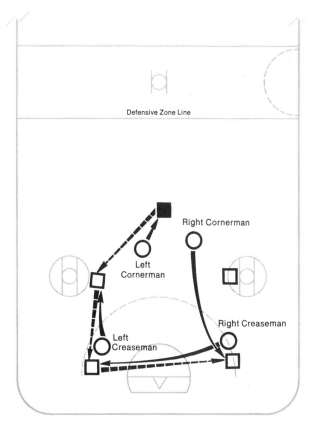

Diagram 35 Man Short — Box Defense — Rotation

Defensive Zone Line

Right Cornerman

Left Cornerman

Right Creaseman

Left Creaseman

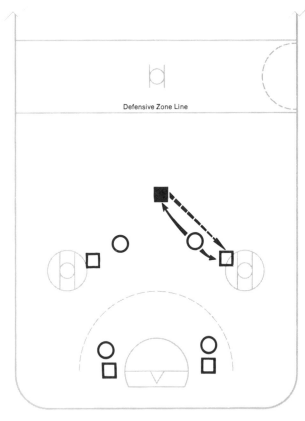

Diagram 36   Man Short — Box Defense —
Creaseman Stationary

offensive creaseman, the opposite defensive creaseman should rotate across and pick up this new ball carrier. If the new ball carrier sees this man rushing him, usually he will pass over to the other offensive creaseman. It is now up to the opposite defensive cornerman to react back and check this ball carrier. All the players have now rotated one position around the box.

In the second method of playing the box, the defensive creasemen hold their positions unless it is absolutely necessary that they react out to stop the offensive cornermen from shooting. Thus, it

Diagram 37   Man Short — Diamond Defense

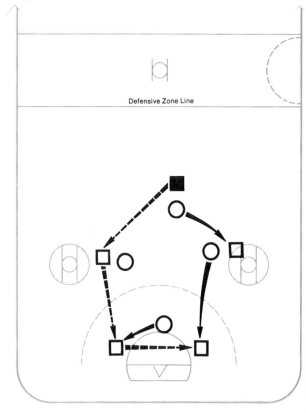

Defensive Zone Line

way or the other, depending upon where the ball is. The defensive creaseman should stand in front of the offensive creaseman, reaching back with his stick on the offensive creaseman's stick. In this way he can keep track of this man and still be in a position to react out to the cornerman. If the offensive cornerman is in a position to shoot, it is the responsibility of the defensive creaseman to stop him from scoring. He does this by rushing out to the shooter and checking him. If the defensive creaseman does react out to the offensive cornerman and he, in turn, passes to the

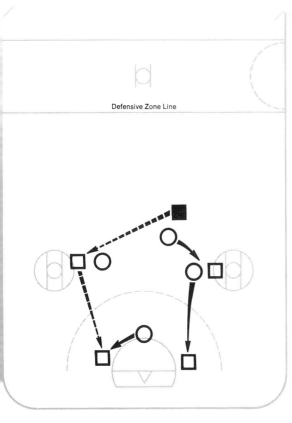

Defensive Zone Line

Diagram 38   Diamond Defense shifting to
             Box Defense

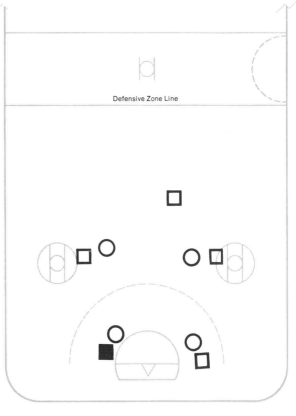

Defensive Zone Line

Diagram 39   Diamond Defense shifted to
             Box Defense

is the duty of the two front men in the box to prevent the three offensive men from getting a good shot on net (*Diagram 36*). This is accomplished by quickly shuffling back and forth trying to get the stick in front of the offensive man's.

Diamond Defense

It is best to use this man-short defense when the power-play players are excellent outside shooters from the point and corners. It is not a good idea to use this defense if the power play has excellent creasemen. Here, one defensive man plays the pointman, two defensive men play the cornermen, and the fourth defensive man plays between the two offensive creasemen (*Diagram 37*). If the ball is thrown to a creaseman, this defensive man must be ready to react to whichever creaseman gets the ball. The offensive creaseman who is in the clear should be picked up by the defensive cornerman reacting back.

A team can effectively rotate from the diamond to the box man short. When the ball is at the point, the man short forms a diamond defense (*Diagram 38*); when the ball is passed to any of the side men (cornermen or creasemen), the diamond rotates, becoming the box defense (*Diagram 39*).

MAN-SHORT OFFENSE

The main objective of the man-short offense is to "kill" or "rag" the ball for two minutes. Once the goalie of the short-handed team has possession of the ball he has two alternatives. 1) He can throw a long pass to one of his two front men breaking. If his breaking teammates are covered closely and he can't pass to them, they should "button hook" (stop quickly and come back) to shake off their checkers and get into the clear for the pass. 2) if his front men are still covered, the goalie can give the ball to one of his defensemen in the crease. The team has only ten seconds to get the ball over the attacking zone line, and once it accomplishes this, the defensive team cannot take it back over this line without losing possession.

The following set play is used to kill the two minutes of the penalty (*Diagram 40*). This play is just a series of screens down one side of the floor and then down the other. To make the play work properly, it is important to use two right shots and two left shots and for them to stay on their own side of the floor. The man-short players keep the same positions (relative to each other) in the attacking zone that they had in the defensive zone. Usually one of the back men will end up with the ball. Just before he becomes double-teamed by the opposition, the back man on the other side of the floor sets a screen for the creaseman on his side of the floor. As this creaseman breaks back toward the attacking zone line, he is given the ball. Now, as he is being double-teamed, the former ball carrier moves to set a screen for the creaseman on his side of the floor. As this creaseman breaks back toward the attacking zone line, he is, in turn, given

the ball. This play continues, hopefully, until the penalty expires. Every now and then a player can use the screen-and-roll to get in the clear for a pass followed by a shot on net. This type of move will keep the defensive players "honest." It is stressed in this system that a player should never take a shot on net while on the man short unless he is absolutely in the clear.

(*Note:* If the proposed rule change comes into effect — that the short-handed team must take a shot on goal

Diagram 40 Man Short — Offense

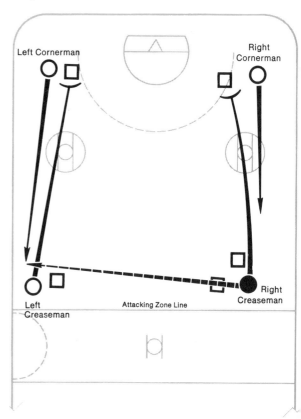

within the thirty-second time limit or lose possession — the man short has to become more offensive minded.

Here, the short-handed team must still try to get the ball into the attacking zone as fast as possible, giving themselves the time needed to set up this special play. The play is executed in the same way as the previous play, except that the ball carrier is more aggressive in trying to work his way into the goal-scoring area so that he will draw two defensive men. As the second defensive player comes in to help his teammate double-team the ball carrier, the ball carrier will then fade back, passing to the creaseman coming off the screen on the other side of the floor. This creaseman, if in the clear, should take a shot on net.

With this new rule, a team shouldn't try to get a shot on net until close to the end of the thirty seconds unless they have a clear-cut shot on net. In the latter case, even if they don't score, they have at least absorbed most of the thirty seconds of the penalty.

If the offensive man-short unit can't get a clear shot on net and the thirty-second limit is almost up, the ball carrier should shoot at the net anyway, hoping for a score or at least a possible rebound off the goalie. If the short-handed team is successful in getting the rebound, the team will be in a position to waste another thirty seconds of the penalty. If the man short doesn't get the rebound, it might be a good idea for the two front men to forecheck in their offensive zone, thus stalling the power-play unit from setting up right away.

It should be noted that the power play must also take a shot on net within thirty seconds or lose possession.)

The goalie sometimes comes up over the attacking zone line to act as a fifth attacker. If he is a scoring threat, he must be checked. This relieves the pressure put on the ball carrier, as there is now only one man checking him. If the goalie is not checked, the ball carrier can use him as a safety-valve when he gets in trouble. If the ball carrier passes the ball to the goaltender, the players shouldn't wait until an opponent gets on him before making the screens. As soon as the goaltender gets the ball, they should get a player in the clear to receive a pass.

Another deceptive play used while on the man short occurs when the goalie feeds a pass up to one of his players. The pass should go to a player who plays on the opposite side of the floor to the players' bench. As one of his teammates enters the defensive door, another breaks out from the attacking door. Usually, this breaking player will be a few feet in front of his checker (as this defensive man was checking the player who just entered the defensive door) and thus will receive the pass from the ball carrier.

7   Face-offs

The importance of face-offs is not emphasized sufficiently by coaches. Obviously, if a team doesn't have the ball, it can't score. Especially in lacrosse, when a team has possession of the ball it has complete control.

CENTERMAN STANCE

To be a good drawman, or centerman, a player must have strong arms and wrists and quick reflexes. Common to all stances, the player stays in a crouched position with knees slightly flexed. Some players like to face toward the opposition's goal (right-hand shot only), having both feet parallel, with the back foot a bit behind the other (*Figure 57, right*) or extended with the foot turned sideways to act as a brace (*Figure 57, left*). Other centermen like to face their opponent

Figure 57

Figure 58

with feet parallel in a wide stance (*Figure 58*). Some players like to kneel when drawing, but this puts the player at a disadvantage as he has to get back onto his feet after picking the ball up.

The centerman draws the way he shoots, and the face-off rule states that the open face of each player's stick must face toward his own goal. The right-hand shot therefore has a slight advantage over the left-hand shot on the fast break from the face-off, as he can face his opponent's goal. The left-hand shot, conversely, must face his own goal (see Figure 57, page 75). Consequently, if he does win the draw, he has to turn around to run toward the opposition's net.

DRAWING ACTION

The rule states that as soon as the referee lets go of the ball between the netting of the two sticks, both players are to draw straight back. A player will often try to get the jump on his opponent by "trapping" the ball under the netting of the stick and then drawing back. But this is illegal and if noticed by the referee will result in a turn-over. Another way a player tries to get the jump on his opponent is by putting his stick forward a little bit so that when the referee places the ball between the two sticks he will have the advantage of more gut on which to draw. The referee is supposed to place the ball exactly in the center between the two sticks, but he sometimes misses this slight variation.

It is legal to draw slightly and then trap. So the best way for a player to get possession is for him to turn his stick as he draws, that is, to draw and trap (*Figure 59*), and end up scooping up the ball. To get as much power as he can on

Figure 59

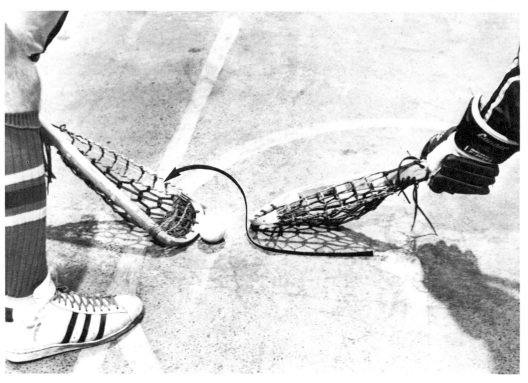

the draw, the centerman should have his top hand as close to the neck of the stick as possible. When he draws, he can put pressure downward as he turns his stick, as well as sideways against his opponent's stick. Another way of draw-

ing is to double-draw. This action consists of pushing the stick slightly forward (*Figure 60*) and then pulling back (*Figure 61*) as you turn the stick completely around (*Figure 62*) to flip the ball back to the defensemen or goalie (*Figure 63*).

Figure 60

Figure 61

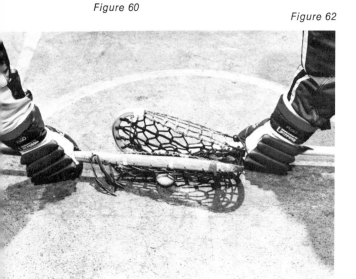

Figure 62

Figure 63

WINNING THE DRAW

In trying to gain control of the ball, some centermen try to draw the ball out between and in front of the legs where they can scoop it up cleanly (*Figure 64*). They should be in the process of standing up as they pick up the ball. After picking up the ball, the centerman should take off toward his opponent's goal. Other centermen like to draw the ball back between the legs where one of the creasemen (not cornermen) can come in behind and scoop it up. Still other centermen, on winning the draw, like to flip or knock the ball back into their defensive zone to the goalie or to a defenseman (see Figures 60-63).

If the ball goes loose from the draw, it is the centerman's job to pursue it wherever it goes and fight for possession. If the centerman has problems in picking the ball up cleanly, he should knock it back to his goalie. In fact, every player should try to pick the ball up cleanly from the face-off, but if he encounters trouble, he should knock the ball back to the goalie.

If the opposition centerman keeps winning the draw and knocking the ball back to his goalie, a method of combating this is to put one of the creasemen halfway between the attacking zone line and the goal. Naturally, a defenseman will go back with him, but at least there will be a fifty-fifty chance of retrieving the ball.

Figure 64

Figure 65

Another method of combating this is to have a creaseman "shoot" in and check the centerman.

FACE-OFF ALIGNMENT

At the center zone face-off circle, each defenseman should line up either with his opponent on the inside of him or on his opponent's stick side. He takes a position on the outside in case the ball rolls toward the boards; this way he has first chance at the ball. The defenseman puts his stick over his opponent's stick so that in case the ball comes his way he can knock his opponent's stick down and pick up the ball.

On the fast break from the center zone face-off, when the centerman gains possession, the two creasemen (who are also on the outside of their men) break toward the boards to draw their checkers. This leaves the center area open for the centerman. The creasemen can then gradually cut back in direct line with the goalie's crease.

On an end zone face-off, every player must make sure he has an opponent, especially if the face-off occurs in his defensive zone (*Figure 65*).

8 Goaltending

The goaltender is the backbone of the defense and the trigger for the fast break. It is important for the goaltender, especially in lacrosse, where there are many goals scored, to realize that the opposition team is going to score on him and that he must not become discouraged when they do or he will psych himself out. Goaltenders must be cocky, confident and daring.

BASIC STANCE

A good goaltender's position is a semi-crouch, with knees bent, back straight, head up and feet about shoulder width apart. If the goalie has his knees bent,

he will be able to move laterally, which is extremely important in goaltending. If he were to stand up straight, his knees would lock, prohibiting him from making this lateral movement. Also, with the knees bent, the goalie will be able to spring up for high shots.

A goalie should hold the stick where the guard meets the stick handle, with the arm slightly bent. Some goalies like to rest the stick between their legs, touching the floor lightly in their ready stance (*Figure 66*). Others prefer to have the stick at their side and slightly in front so that it can be moved quickly, without impediment, to either side of the body to make stick saves. But during play, goaltenders will vary the position of the

Figure 66

stick from the front to the side, depending on where the ball is headed.

The goalie's free hand should be resting near his thigh with the palm facing out. Some goaltenders like to have a pad on the back of this free hand to deflect shots. This stance may vary slightly according to the style of the goaltender and the type of shot.

DEFENDING THE NET

During the passing of the ball back and forth amongst the offensive players, the goaltender should be following the ball with his body as well as his eyes and concentrating on staying mentally in the game, ready for anything. The goalie, besides keeping his eyes on the ball at all times, should know the positions on the floor of the dangerous offensive players. Then he will know what to expect as a result of a quick pass from one side of the floor to the other. In addition to stopping balls, starting fast breaks and gathering loose balls, a good goalie will make sure his teammates are also mentally in the game by yelling at them to let them know if there are any offensive players unchecked or in the clear.

Figure 67

Playing the Long Shot

The most important thing for a goal-tender to do in stopping most shots is to play the angles to the goal. By playing the angles correctly he can save himself unnecessary work. For the goaltender to play the long shot, he must concentrate on the player's stick (not his body) in order to get his own angle to the goal. The farther the goaltender moves out in his crease, the more he cuts down on the target, forcing the shooter to go for the more difficult corners (*Figure 67*). But in playing the angles a goalie must always remember that he cannot rely strictly on his floor or crease position to stop the ball; no matter how well he plays the angle, there are still many openings, and he must be ready with stick, arms, legs and body to make reflex saves.

It is wise for the goalie to remember that he has to be out and set before the shot is taken, as a goalie has difficulty moving laterally when he is in the process of moving forward. As the goalie moves out on the shooter he should always know where the net is, either by reaching back with his stick or free hand to find the post or by judging from his position with the crease. Even when the ball carrier is in the corner of the arena, the goalie should still move out on the crease to cut down the angle. A goalie should try to play all long, low shots with his stick and all long, high shots mainly with his chest.

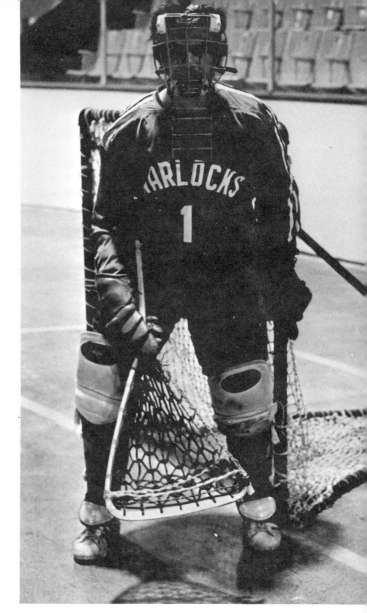

Figure 68

Playing the Crease or Close-in Shot

A goaltender, in playing a crease shot, must be careful not to make the first

move. If the ball carrier starts from the side of the net, the goalie's foot should rest on the inside of the short side post (*Figure 68*). If the ball carrier continues to cut across in front of the net, the goalie must move with the shooter in order to cover the angle. The goalie must not over-guard the net, but should move out slightly and be set to move laterally. Here, the anticipation of the goalie is very important. He should make it inviting for the shooter to shoot where he would like him to shoot (by giving him an opening at which to shoot), thereby anticipating the shot (*Figure 69*). If it is a high shot, a goalie should try to take it off his chest (*Figure 70*).

Most goalies find that left-handed shooters have a tendency to shoot to the left side of the net, or to the goalie's right side, and vice-versa for right-handed players.

Figure 69

Figure 70

Playing the Bounce Shot

The most difficult shot for a goalie to handle is the bounce shot. The best way to block a bounce shot is to attack it at almost the point of impact where the ball meets or bounces off the playing surface. Ideally, the stick should be used to catch the ball before it bounces, but this is not always possible, and as it is extremely difficult to judge the angle and speed of a bounce shot, the stick should always be backed up with as much of the body as possible. If trying to catch the ball fails, the goalie should react to the ball and try to smother it.

Figure 71

This just means moving into the bounce with the legs close together (*Figure 71*). A goaltender should always stay on his feet until the shot has been taken; he should never drop to the knees to block a bounce shot (or any shot) until he sees where the shot is going (*Figure 72*). In stopping all types of shots, don't guess.

Playing the Breakaway

Three or four times in a game, a goalie will find himself faced with a breakaway situation. At least here a goalie has no screens or deflections to worry about. As was discussed, he should give the shooter something to shoot at. Again, anticipation is stressed, but without the aspect of over-commitment. As the shooter comes in close, the scoring area of the net is diminished. His greatest asset when he is close to the net is his stick fake, which should now be foreseen by the goalie.

Loose Balls and Rebounds

Loose balls are an important part of the game, and a goalie can be a great asset in this department. When the ball is at the other end of the arena, the goaltender should move out about twenty-five feet from his crease to pick up any

Figure 72

Figure 73

Figure 74

loose balls that may stray back. When his team is on defense the goalie can make himself very helpful by retrieving any loose balls around the net and by recovering rebounds. On any face-off, but mainly in his own zone, a goaltender should stand just outside his own crease. In this way, his centerman or any other player who gets in trouble can knock the ball back to him and won't be called for passing the ball into the crease.

THE GOALTENDER AS AN OFFENSIVE WEAPON

1) The goaltender can start the fast break by throwing a short, quick pass to either a cornerman or a pointman. The goalie must be as accurate a passer as any other player on the team (*Figure 73*).

2) If the fast break starts to lag, it is up to the goalie to pick the right time and break up the floor with the ball, eventually passing it off. This type of move should pick up the pace of the game, as it is very embarrassing to the other players if the goalie "outlegs" them. Perhaps the goalie can even draw an opponent and then pass off, creating an extra man down the floor (*Figure 74*).

3) The goalie can also be very effective in throwing a long, arcing pass to one of his fast-breaking forwards (*Figure 75*). The teammate should break down the side, then curve to the center of the floor, where he should contact the long pass with his stick over his shoulder (see Figure 4, page 5).

If a player happens to break down the middle of the floor, it is better for him to receive the pass over the head, with the

Figure 75

stick held out in front of his body, rather than over his shoulder (see Figure 6, page 7). It is essential for the goalie to time the arcing lead pass to coincide with the speed of the breaker.

Figure 76

4) It was mentioned how important it is that the goalie be able to pass as well as the other players. Naturally, it will make the offense more potent if the goalie is also able to score goals (*Figure 76*). As the goalie starts his run down the floor with the ball, he might end up taking it all the way, with an eventual shot on net.

5) An offensive goalie can also be very useful to a team when both teams have been penalized with a minor penalty. The goalie can now move up offensively to play the point or corner position as the fifth man on the power play. The goalie should start the power play by trying to draw one of the defensive players out of position. Naturally, as soon as he passes off, he should react back toward his net. If there is a shot on the opposition's net, each player must pick up his man to stop the opposing team from getting a shot on their open net.

A "BOOK" ON OPPONENTS

Another very important job for the goaltender is to keep a "book" on all opposing players. A good goalie should know how opposing players carry the ball, how they shoot (sidearm, underarm, fakes) and their favorite moves. This is very important, as most players have a favorite shot which they invariably use when under pressure. The more knowledge the goalkeeper has of each opposition player's style, the greater will be his chances of stopping the ball in any given situation.

9 Drills for the Fast-Break, Short-Pass System

PASSING AND CATCHING DRILLS

Most players feel that they can pass well enough and that practice in passing is a waste of time. If a player can pass the ball quickly and crisply into another player's stick ten out of ten times, only then is he a good passer.

1. Individual Passing Drill

This drill could be done on the practice floor but is more beneficial if done on one's own. All a player does is find a wall and start banging the ball against it. Being alone, a player is able to concentrate on what he is doing wrong and on his shooting accuracy. To improve his accuracy he simply picks a particular spot on the wall and tries to hit it with the ball. Later on, he might draw a four-foot square from the ground up to represent a lacrosse net and shoot at the corners.

2. Stationary Pair Passing Drill

This simply consists of having two stationary players pass a ball back and forth. Here, the coach should keep stressing that the ball be thrown in the correct way.

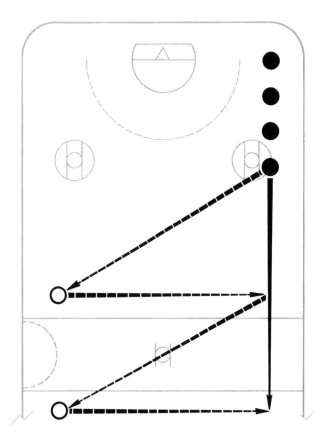

Diagram 41   Individual Player
Passing-on-the-Run Drill

the first passer, breaks, gets the return pass and automatically passes to the second passer, breaks and gets the return pass to end up with a shot on net. Work this drill from both sides of the floor.

4. Speed Passing Drill

In the next drill the players form lines extending down both sides of the arena floor, with each player facing a partner. The first player in one of the lines has a bucket of balls beside him. He passes

Diagram 42   Speed Passing Drill

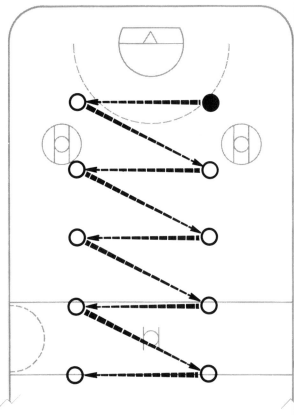

3. Individual Player Passing-on-the-Run Drill

This drill gives each player a chance to practice while on the run the in-and-out motion of the ball in the stick which is so important in the fast-break system. Players are positioned, one at a time, at the attacking zone line and at the defensive zone line. The rest of the squad lines up in a single file, each player with a ball, at one end of the arena (*Diagram 41*). The first player in the line passes to each ball to the player across from him, who in turn, passes back across to the player beside the original passer (*Diagram 42*). The ball goes back and forth in this zig-zag fashion until it reaches the end of the line. The player at the end of the line will put all the balls in the empty bucket beside him.

The coach should note which players drop the ball. After all the balls have been thrown, these players must run once around the arena for each time they dropped a ball.

The coach should put pressure on the players by recording their progress. This is done by timing, with a stopwatch, how long it takes for one ball to go all the way down the line. Improvement should be stressed each time.

5. Pair Passing-on-the-Run Drill

In this drill all the right-handed shots are in one line and all the left-handed shots in the other. A right- and a left-handed shot pair up and throw as many passes as possible on the run to the other end of the arena (*Diagram 43*). The ball carrier should jog at first, but after he has passed the ball, he should break two or three steps and receive the ball in top flight. The player who ends up with the ball closest to the net takes the shot.

INDIVIDUAL OFFENSIVE AND DEFENSIVE DRILLS

1. Shuffle Drill

This is just a sideways sliding movement of the feet, used on defense while checking a ball carrier. In this drill the players shuffle in the direction the coach indicates. It should be stressed that the feet must not be crossed.

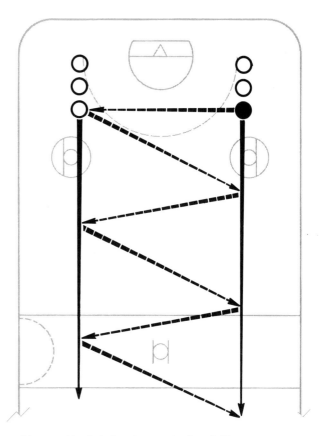

Diagram 43   Pair Passing-on-the-Run Drill

2. One-on-One Drill

The players practice their offensive and defensive moves. They form a shooting line and a checking line. Each offensive player tries to beat the defensive player for a shot on net. The players rotate to the opposite line when the play is finished.

3. Chasing Drill

This is probably one of the hardest drills of all. Starting with about one and a half feet between them, a player chases a ball carrier, on the whistle, from one end zone face-off circle to the other end of the floor, trying to stop him from taking a shot on net. When the players get to the other end, they switch positions and run back.

This drill is used for three main reasons:

1) for conditioning, both physically and mentally. When a ball carrier gets ahead of a player, many times the player gives up trying to catch him. This drill gives the chaser the positive mental attitude that he can catch a player who gets ahead of him in a game.

2) for hurrying the shot. Even if the chaser doesn't catch the ball carrier, he can prevent him from having the time he wants to fake and shoot at the goalie.

3) for teaching players not to cross-check from behind. Checking from behind usually results in a penalty, a possession call or possibly a penalty shot. This drill stops a player from hitting the panic button. Now, when a ball carrier gets in front and can't be caught, the defensive player learns to wait until the ball carrier pulls back, or "cocks," his stick to shoot and then checks his stick (see Figure 30, page 20).

LOOSE BALL DRILLS

1. Loose Ball Drill

This drill gives players practice in taking a check while picking up a loose ball. The players form two lines at the attacking zone line. The coach then rolls the ball into the corner. On the whistle, the first two players in each line run for the ball. If the ball rests beside the boards, the first player to the ball has to brace himself to take a check and, at the same time, pick up the ball. He can do this 1) by putting one hand against the boards, while using his body as a shield, and picking the ball up with his other hand or 2) by bending his back low enough so that the check will ride up over his back or 3) by leaning slightly back to absorb the check as he is hit and then picking up the ball using both hands on the stick.

If the ball rebounds off the boards, the second man in should wait until the first man goes to pick it up, then knock his stick either up or down and quickly retrieve the ball. The player who gets the ball becomes the offensive player and the other player becomes the defensive player. They are now in a one-on-one situation.

2. Scoop Drill

Four or five players line up in the middle of the floor facing the side boards (*Diagram 44*). The first man who has the ball runs in and bounces it off the boards. As soon as the ball hits the boards, the next man should react by charging the ball and catching it. This is not only a pickup drill but also encourages the players to go to the ball rather than wait for it to come to them.

SHOOTING DRILLS

1. Shooting Contest

Many times it is nice to end the practices with a bit of fun. This can be

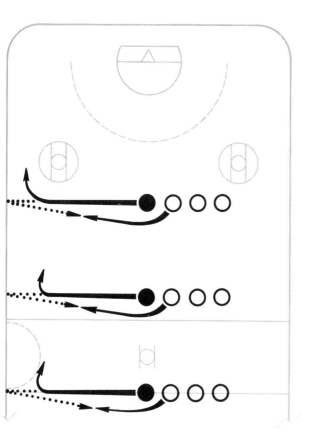

Diagram 44 Scoop Drill

GOALTENDING DRILLS

Shooting drills and goaltending drills are the same drills. The difference is that when the coach wants to emphasize the shooting aspect, he will point out the shooter's mistakes, but when he wants to emphasize goaltending drills, he will tell the players what type of shot to take and where to shoot so that these particular shots will help the goaltender to correct his weaknesses.

1. Single Line Drill

All the players, each with a ball, line up at center in a single file, then one after another in rapid succession, they run in on net and shoot.

2. Semicircle Drill

The players form a semicircle along the free-throw line. Starting at one end, the players fire, one after another, in rapid succession.

3. Corner Drill

All the left-hand shooters go into the right corner and all the right-hand shooters go into the left corner. Alternately, the players run across in front of the net, shooting at the goalie's weakest spot.

4. Crease Drill

This drill helps an offensive crease-man to practice taking a pass on the crease and then stepping out in front of the goalie for a better shot (see Power Play, page 61). Four lines are formed, a

accomplished by getting two players to choose teams for a shooting contest. The players from each team will shoot at the goalie alternately, one at a time, until one team gets twenty-one points. Three points are given for a score from outside the free-throw line, but it has to be made with a bounce shot; two points are given for a long shot from outside the free-throw line; and one point is given for any other type of shot.

passing and shooting line consisting of only right-hand shots and a passing and shooting line consisting of only left-hand shots. A right-handed passer standing near the face-off circle will pass to a left-handed shot on the crease (*Diagram 45*). This man will take the pass, then the step out for the shot. The pass should be alternated from the right to the left, with the players rotating from the passing to the shooting line.

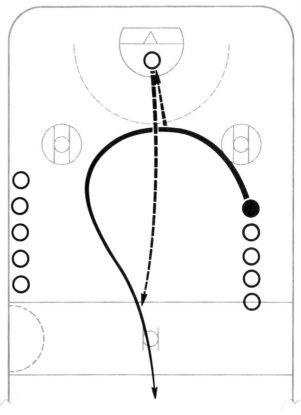

Diagram 46   Goaltender's Passing Drill

Diagram 45   Crease Drill

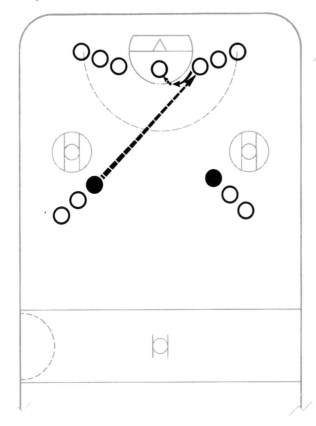

5. Goaltender's Passing Drill

The players, each with a ball, form two lines (of left-handed and right-handed shots, on their wrong sides), facing the goalie. The player makes a semicircular run, rolling his ball in to the goalie, then continues his run down his proper side of the floor to receive the long, lobbing pass from the goalie as he nears the center area (*Diagram 46*).

FAST-BREAK SYSTEM DRILLS

1. Odd-Man Drills

In practicing these odd-man situations, execute them under pressure 1) by putting a count on them or 2) by delaying a defensive man at the defensive zone line for a few seconds before he can get back into play and nullify the odd-man play.

Start with the two-on-one play, then from the center zone face-off circle, run the three-on-two play as if it were an actual face-off situation. Run the four-on-three from around the center face-off circle, then run the five-on-four, but from the defensive zone. The break-out pattern should be stressed first, before the actual five-on-four play is completed in the attacking zone.

OFFENSIVE TEAM DRILLS

1. The Give-and-Go Drill

This drill consists of four groups of players: the right-handed shots form a checking line and a passing line on one side of the floor, while on the other side of the floor the left-handed shots form a checking line and a shooting line. The drill starts with the shooter throwing to the passer. If the passer is being checked closely, he should fake down and come back quickly to get the outside pass from the shooter. After passing, the shooter fakes his checker to the outside and breaks to the center, in front of his checker, for a return pass (*Diagram 47*). It is a good habit to get the passer to follow in behind the shooter for any rebounds. This drill can be worked from both sides of the floor.

2. The Screen Drill

This drill consists of four groups of left-handed players and two groups of right-handed players. The left-handed

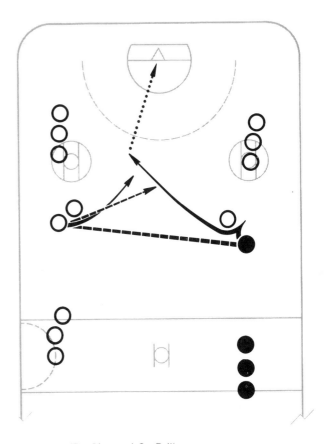

Diagram 47   Give-and-Go Drill

cornerman passes the ball over to the opposite cornerman, who in turn, passes to the creaseman. The left-handed cornerman sets a screen for his creaseman, who gets the pass from his opposite

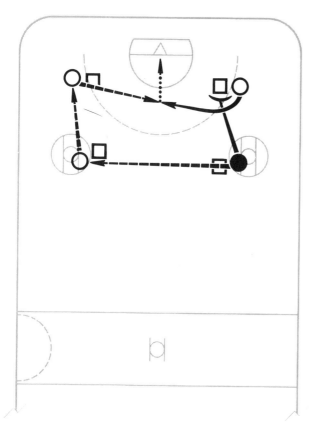

Diagram 48 Screen Drill

creaseman (*Diagram 48*). This drill can be worked from both sides of the floor.

The pivot-screen and the screen-and-roll can be worked the same way.

3. The Pick-and-Roll Drill

Usually the cornerman and creaseman from the same line pair up to practice this play. With checkers, either the cornerman or creaseman picks, depending on who has the ball. If the cornerman has the ball, then the creaseman picks for him, and vice versa.

10 Statistics for the Fast-Break, Short-Pass System

PURPOSE

Most people think of statistics as simply a record of how many goals and assists an individual player has accumulated. However, most of the statistics that are taken in a lacrosse game involve more than simple scores. Some of the more general lacrosse statistics which are taken are: loose balls, shots on goal by check, face-offs and giveaways.

A coach should generally examine stats for the purpose of getting an overall picture of how a game or a period was played and the major weaknesses in the team. It is important to note that statistics will not always indicate which team won the game, but may simply be an indication of how the game was played.

The Windsor Warlocks and Oshawa Green Gaels use three basic sheets to compile their statistics. Two sheets are used during the game, and the summary sheet is compiled from the other two sheets. Also, these summary sheets are kept for an accumulated summary sheet as the season progresses.

FIRST SHEET   (*Diagram 49*)

Loose Balls

It would be fair to state that loose balls are the most important statistic for the coach. A loose ball occurs when two opposing players contest for a stray ball. If the player retrieves it, he gets credit for it; if he doesn't get it, then he doesn't get credit. At the end of each game or period, loose balls are expressed as a comparison of how many loose balls the player was credited with and the total number of loose balls the player had a chance at. Example: 3/5 means a player had five chances at loose balls and was credited with collecting three of them.

Diagram 49

WINDSOR WARLOCKS SENIOR LACROSSE CLUB -- STATISTICS

Windsor vs. __WESTVILLE__   Period __1__   Date_____

Player	Loose Balls By Windsor	By Opponents	Shots Wide	Shots on Goal By Windsor	By Opponents
Moore	///	//	///	/// ① 1-0 ① 2-1 ① 5-5	// ① 1-1

FACE-OFFS

Windsor Center	Opposition Center							Totals
	#19	#5	#6					
Moore	WW	OPP	W					3/4
Technical Infraction								

Windsor vs. *WESTVILLE*_____ Period___*1*___ Date_____

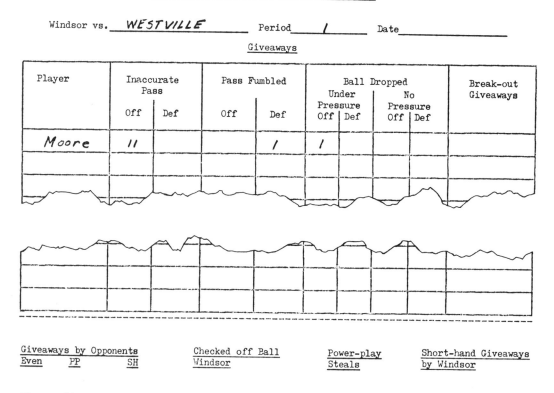

Player	Inaccurate Pass		Pass Fumbled		Ball Dropped				Break-out Giveaways
					Under Pressure		No Pressure		
	Off	Def	Off	Def	Off	Def	Off	Def	
Moore	*II*			*I*	*I*				

Giveaways by Opponents
Even   PP   SH

Checked off Ball
Windsor

Power-play
Steals

Short-hand Giveaways
by Windsor

Diagram 50

Loose balls are a good indication of the aggressiveness and hustle of a team or an individual player.

Shots

There are three different classifications of shots:

1. Shots Wide

This is simply any shot a player takes that does not end up on goal.

2. Shots on Goal

This section includes both the goals scored and the shots on goal by a player during the period. If the player scores, the notch or shot mark is simply circled. It is also important for the coach to know how the goal was scored, whether it was scored on a one-on-one, an odd-man situation (2-on-1, 3-on-2, 4-on-3, 5-on-4), a give-and-go or a screen.

3. Shots on Goal by Check

This is probably the most controversial statistic, because a player obviously doesn't like to be charged with goals, particularly if the goaltender allows a "soft" goal in. Again, as well as showing, by means of a circle, who is charged with the goal, it shows how the goal was scored. In other words, a one-on-one goal (1-1) is entered when a player definitely tries to beat his opponent and scores, while a five-on-five goal (5-5) is given when a player scores on a long shot.

This stat reveals a player's defensive ability. If his check gets many shots on net or goals, the coach will certainly know he isn't doing his share of the work on defense.

Face-offs

Although this record shows centerman against centerman for face-offs, wins or credit are given as the line wins rather than to an individual player. In other words, every man on the line has the responsibility of getting the ball in order to be given credit for the face-off. Doing face-offs in this manner provides a good indication of the team's aggressiveness in a particular game.

This is the next most important thing to loose balls. Face-offs are in fact just another form of a loose ball. The team that controls the face-offs will, to some degree, control the game.

SECOND SHEET — GIVEAWAYS

The giveaway sheet (*Diagram 50*) is pretty well self-explanatory (inaccurate pass, pass fumbled, ball dropped). It is interesting to note that giveaway totals will be a reflection of the team's style of play. For example, the Windsor Warlocks are a running team and thus have more turn-overs (usually between 30 and 38 per game) than a team such as the Peterborough Lakers, who play a more controlled type of game.

THIRD SHEET — SUMMARY

After each game, this sheet (*Diagram 51*) is prepared from the totals of all the statistics taken during each period of the game.

Any number of statistics can be added as the coach sees fit. The important thing in drawing up any statistics sheet is to remain flexible so that it will be easy to add statistics. For example, some coaches like to know who gives up the ball when the team is a man short or who steals the ball when the team is at a man advantage.

Diagram 51

WINDSOR WARLOCKS SENIOR LACROSSE CLUB -- STATISTICS

SUMMARY SHEET   DATE_____

PLAYER	GP	G	A	TP	PIM	TURN-OVERS	LB	SHOTS WIDE	SHOTS ON GOAL	SHOTS BY CHECK S.O.G.	GOALS	FACE-OFFS A W %	
Moore	1	3	2	5	4	4	3/5	3	6	3	1	4 3 15%	

11 Practices

A COACH'S OBJECTIVES IN PRACTICE

A coach should be aware of and understand his players' objectives as well as his own and should be flexible enough to compromise between these two goals.

1) A good coach will help each player to reach his own maximum potential. He should never let the player accept his present level of attainment but should insist that he constantly try to improve and perfect his skills and plays. This is where dedication and self-discipline should be instilled into the players.

2) Self-confidence is one of the most important things with which a coach can help a player. A coach who encourages and reinforces with positive feedback will end up with a player who has a positive attitude toward himself; whereas if a coach bawls a player out for every mistake, the player will begin to doubt his own playing ability. A player who is afraid to do anything for fear of making mistakes and being yelled at will certainly not improve his game.

3) In trying to perfect his players' skills, a coach must be able to analyze their strengths and weaknesses. Perfecting these basic skills will give the players more time to concentrate on their team play.

Also, by teaching the proper methods of performing skills, the coach will keep the players' frustration levels down. For example, if a player doesn't know how to cross-check properly, he will be frustrated by having the players go around him or by getting penalties for using unacceptable methods to stop them. On the other hand, if the player is taught the right way to cross-check, he will probably get fewer penalties and his aggressive effort will be rewarded by his success in stopping the offensive player.

4) A coach should allot a great deal of practice time to the perfection of plays. In the fast-break, short-pass system, each player is designated to run to a specific area; therefore, for the time-precision plays to work, everyone must know where he is supposed to go and what he is supposed to do. The coach should stress that every player attend all practices in order to learn and work on these plays.

Out of the striving for perfection comes self-discipline, as each player disciplines himself to run to his specific position. At the same time, however, the coach must see to it that the players remain flexible enough in their thinking so that they will not always follow the same pattern automatically, as the plays will vary according to the breaks and openings of the game.

5) A coach should also help a player to learn how to control his anger. If a player loses his temper, he will decrease his thinking ability and increase his chances of getting a penalty. Since anger is learned, a coach can and should train his players to control their anger in stressful situations. He does this by giving positive feedback to a controlled response to a situation that would usually arouse anger.

6) A coach must also help a player to learn to handle stress. During a game, in which there is the pressure and tension of competition, a player will sometimes "choke." A coach can help his players by putting pressure on them in practice (having them execute drills intensely, with defensive pressure) so that they acquire the poise and looseness to take advantage of breaks and openings which occur during a game.

7) Lastly, a coach should help a player to get as much out of playing as possible. Naturally, winning is important and is the main objective of most coaches, players and teams. But winning should not be the ultimate goal. How one goes about winning makes the difference. If good sportsmanship and personal integrity are destroyed for the sake of winning, then the importance of winning is being overemphasized. If players are pushed to the point where the fun is taken out of the game and the practices, for the sake of winning, then winning isn't important. Players must be taught that the extrinsic reward of winning is not as satisfying as the intrinsic reward of knowing one has played his hardest and his best.

There is also the experience of playing on a team. Working and suffering together with other individuals in an effort to win should bring lasting friendships which no material thing can replace.

SETTING UP A PRACTICE

A good practice is the best environment to motivate an athlete to perform at his best.

Athletes want to play the game, but they usually dislike practicing. It should be the goal of all coaches to make the practices interesting, challenging and fun for the players. The practices should be well organized and fast moving so that the players are busy and participating and no time is wasted. The practice should not be allowed to become routine and dull, but should be varied so that the players will stay eager and interested.

If the coach is enthusiastic during the practice, he will find that his enthusiasm will spread to the players, which will help to keep up the tempo of the practice.

Athletes need to be pushed to get the most out of them. Therefore, the coach must emphasize hard work in his practices and the importance of being in top physical condition. Hard practices will make a player mentally and physically tough.

Warm-ups

Warm-ups are mainly for conditioning and consist mostly of jogging and short, quick "bursts." Some coaches feel warm-ups prevent injuries and prepare the players for physical contact.

Figure 77

Calisthenics

Calisthenics are mainly done to get the players physically in shape for the season. Exercises are done to strengthen certain muscles which are used extensively in lacrosse. These muscles will involve the legs, arms and stomach. A lot of stretching exercises are also done to cut down on pulled or torn muscles (Figure 77).

Calisthenics should be done for the first few months and then gradually dropped after the season begins. Otherwise, they become dragged out unnecessarily.

Talk by the Coach

This talk should be brief. He should talk about the purpose of the particular practice and what they are going to work on and why, and some of the major points of the last game.

Skill

Before the coach introduces the skill, he should make sure the learning environment is good, *i.e.,* every player is paying complete attention and there are no distractions in the arena. Players learn better when they are fresh and mentally alert, so it is better to have the teaching of skills close to the start of the practice.

The coach should first demonstrate the skill, making sure everyone can see. His instructions should be brief and clear, stressing the major points so that the players will remember them. He should ask questions periodically to make sure the players understand what he is talking about. When he feels they have a pretty good knowledge of the skill and what is expected of them, he should let them practice the skill on their own. Here, they will get the intrinsic feedback (feeling of doing it right) which is so important in learning a skill.

The coach goes around making individual corrections to players who are performing the skill the wrong way. In making these corrections the coach should give positive performance feedback, *i.e.,* he shouldn't tell the player he is doing it wrong, but should explain to him that if he tried it another way he might get better results. Video-tape replays are an excellent method of correcting skills, as the players get immediate visual feedback.

Drills

Once the players start to execute the skill correctly, the coach should put it in a drill situation. He should first explain the purpose of the drill and how it is related to the game. It is better for the players to understand the whole, then break it down into parts, *i.e.,* learn the whole fast-break system first by diagram, then break it down into parts (two-on-one, three-on-two, etc.). A variety of drills in short bouts are more effective than long drills, as they keep the players interested and motivated. Drills should duplicate game conditions whenever possible. This means that plays and skills should be rehearsed at the speed at which they will be used during the game.

Execution of plays and skills at an intense pace will put stress and pressure on the players as they try to perform them correctly. Under pressure, players will go back to their old habits, whether these habits are right or wrong. So it is very important for the coach to correct any mistakes during practice and make sure the habits formed are the right ones. In teaching skillful plays, stress and pressure should not be added immediately. For example, shooting drills should be conducted in the absence of defensive interference. As the play is acquired, the pressure of a defensive player should be added. Eventually, the defensive player will start to check, becoming more and more aggressive until an actual game situation is simulated.

Team Strategy

This usually involves practicing the five-on-five situation, *i.e.,* an offensive unit against a defensive unit. This is a controlled situation, with emphasis on the offense or defense, depending on what the coach wants to work on. The coach, on beginning certain offensive or defensive plays, may want the players to walk through the play or at least practice it slowly at first until all the players who are involved in the play know what to do. Eventually, the play will be tried at game speed with game conditions so that the players can work on their timing. Most of the major factors that apply to the drills apply here.

Scrimmages

Scrimmages usually take place close to the end of the practice. Again, scrimmages should be controlled, *i.e.,* players should be stopped on the whistle so that the coach can go over what has happened. Here, the coach can see whether the players have applied the skills and plays they have been previously practicing.

Conditioning

For a player to play in the fast-break system, he must have a high level of endurance. It is a known fact that players quit mentally before they do physically. Those players who are in shape won't quit as soon and as easily as those who are out of shape. Having this high level of endurance helps them to adapt to pain, resist fatigue and recover quickly from fatigue.

The problem with conditioning exercises designed to produce this high level of endurance is that many of them are monotonous and uninteresting. Therefore, the coach is faced with the task of motivating his players into getting into shape. The main technique used to achieve this is to camouflage the conditioning. A coach can make certain that in all the warm-ups and drills there is some running involved so that the conditioning factor is present. It is certainly more fun to run throwing the ball or checking a player than to run for running's sake.

Lacrosse requires the ability to run consistently throughout the whole game and to break out periodically with short bursts of power. The best way to train for both is to do interval training. This consists of about ten work bouts of less than one minute's duration, running at maximum intensity (approximately two or three times around the floor) with a short rest period (not complete recovery). A coach will have to experiment with the timing of the work bouts and rest periods.

Sometimes, just for variety, a coach can do starts-and-stops and wind-sprint drills at the end of the practice, but to do this in every practice is mentally fatiguing and boring. Never underestimate the value of running relay races to help stimulate interest in conditioning.

Warm-downs

After a strenuous practice, have the players jog around the arena three or four times until they get their breathing back to normal.

SELECTION OF PLAYERS THROUGH PRACTICES

Although the final decision on whether or not to keep a player should be made when he is playing in a game, practices give a good indication of a player's make-up. The attitude of a player is important in this fast-break, hard-running system. Thus, the players are pushed hard in the early practices to see if they have any intestinal fortitude, *i.e.,* an unwillingness to quit when they get a little tired. Many good potential players have been cut because of a lackadaisical attitude. Players who loaf or cheat during the warm-ups and calisthenics or try to avoid these exercises because of minor injuries will usually quit when the going gets tough. The hustling and aggressive sort of player is sought because he usually possesses the *desire to win*. One of the last things to look for in a player is whether or not he can handle a stick. If a player has the desire, a willingness to work and a sense of dedication, he cannot fail to improve his technique.

Lacrosse is a great game and a player will get out of it what he puts into it.